STANDARDS EXEMPLAR SERIES

Assessing
Student Performance
Grades 9–12

STANDARDS EXEMPLAR SERIES

Assessing
Student Performance
Grades 9–12

Edited by
Miles Myers
and Elizabeth Spalding

National Council of Teachers of English
1111 W. Kenyon Road, Urbana, IL 61801-1096

Grateful acknowledgment is made to the following publishers and agencies for permission to use materials from their publications:

Pages xii–xiii and 11–14: From *NAEP 1992 Writing Report Card,* by Arthur N. Applebee, Judith A. Langer, Ina V. S. Mullis, Andrew S. Latham, and Claudia A. Gentile (Report No. 23-W01, June 1994); *Reading Assessment Redesigned: Authentic Texts and Innovative Instruments in NAEP's 1992 Survey,* by Judith A. Langer, Jay R. Campbell, Susan B. Neuman, Ina V. S. Mullis, Hilary R. Persky, and Patricia L. Donahue (Report No. 23-FR-07, January 1995); and *Grammar, Punctuation, and Spelling: Controlling the Conventions of Written English at Ages 9, 13, and 17,* by Arthur N. Applebee, Judith A. Langer, and Ina V. S. Mullis (Report No. 15–W03, June 1987). NAEP is a congressionally mandated project of the National Center for Education Statistics of the U.S. Department of Education. NAEP reports are prepared for the Office of Educational Research and Improvement of the U.S. Department of Education by the Educational Testing Service, Princeton, New Jersey, under contract with the National Center for Education Statistics.

Pages 2–5 and 28–30: From *A Sampler of English-Language Arts Assessment: High School* (1994). Permission granted by the California Department of Education.

Pages 15–19 and 113–114, 116: Reprinted with permission from *Twelve Thousand Students and Their English Teachers: Tested Units in Teaching Literature, Language, Composition.* Copyright ©1968 by College Entrance Examination Board. All rights reserved.

Pages 20–23 and 109–112: Reprinted with permission from *End-of-Year Examinations in English for College-Bound Students Grades 9–12.* Copyright ©1963 by College Entrance Examination Board. All rights reserved.

Page 40: Rubric for breadth of reading adapted from *New Standards 1995–96: Middle Grades English Language Arts Portfolio* (1995) with the permission of the New Standards™.

Book Coordinator: Maria Drees

NCTE Stock Number: 47011-3050

It is the policy of NCTE in its journals and other publications to provide a forum for the open discussion of ideas concerning the content and the teaching of English and the language arts. Publicity accorded to any particular point of view does not imply endorsement by the Executive Committee, the Board of Directors, or the membership at large, except in announcements of policy, where such endorsement is clearly specified.

Although every attempt is made to ensure accuracy at the time of publication, NCTE cannot guarantee that published electronic mail addresses are current.

Library of Congress Cataloging-in-Publication Data
Myers, Miles.
    Exemplar series / Miles Myers and Elizabeth Spalding.
        p.   cm.
    ISBN 0–8141–4698–8 (v. 1 : pbk.). —ISBN 0–8141–4700–3 (v. 2 : pbk.). — ISBN 0–8141–4701–1 (v. 3 : pbk.)
    1. Language arts—Ability testing—United States. 2. English language—Ability testing—United States. 3. Portfolios in education—United States. 4. Language arts—Standards—United States. I. Spalding, Elizabeth, 1951– . II. Title.
LB1576.M943   1997
    428'.0076—dc21   96-47771
                                                                    CIP

Contents

Foreword

Are you looking for some way to show your students your goals and standards? This book will help you do that and more. The contents of this book grew out of the work of thousands of classroom teachers across the country who worked together to design on-demand tasks and portfolios to assess, among other things, the contents of the *Standards for the English Language Arts* (SELA), which were formulated by the National Council of Teachers of English and the International Reading Association.

The first key point to be made here is that this publication has been a large-group effort. Except for the introduction and some editing work on task descriptions, rubrics, and commentaries, the editors have been largely traffic engineers. The on-demand tasks and portfolio entries selected for this publication were originally developed by teachers working in various state projects (e.g., California, Kentucky), in various national assessment projects (e.g., College Board, National Assessment of Educational Progress), and in various curriculum projects sponsored by NCTE. Teachers who have worked in these projects will find that their original work has been modified or added to during the review and piloting process.

The second key point is that the on-demand tasks and portfolios in this publication were selected because they clearly illustrated in some way how the standards for the English language arts appear in typical classroom assignments and typical student performance. The tasks were often selected because they focused on frequently assigned literary selections and frequently assigned writing topics. Some of these tasks and portfolio entries have been "standard" for two dozen years, and some have become "standard" in recent years. The on-demand tasks and portfolio entries were also selected because the student performance, although not the very best or the very worst, was representative of the range from high to low.

The third key point is that the selections presented here are a limited sample of what is needed to assess the content of English language arts. The assessment of the standards for the English language arts requires a wide range of information—on-demand tasks, portfolio entries, multiple-choice tests, and teacher judgments of discussions and oral presentations. Multiple-choice tests and teacher judgments of discussions and oral presentations are not presented in this publication. This publication displays responses at different levels to on-demand tasks—the exemplars in the first section—and portfolio entries —the exemplars in the second section. On-demand tasks are assignments used across many classrooms, almost always with time limitations, and the portfolios are a combination of assigned and freely chosen projects, timed and untimed. On-demand tasks focus on particular standards and allow us to make comparisons across classes and districts. Portfolio entries usually tell us something unique about how each student achieves the English standards, providing evidence of how a student develops an idea over time, how several performances interact, how the student reflects about his or her work, and what the student emphasizes when allowed to make choices. We hope the exemplars—the on-demand tasks and the portfolios—will illuminate further the processes involved in achieving the NCTE/IRA standards and contribute to the ongoing conversations these standards have initiated. We want to thank all of the teachers who contributed to this project through their work on assessments across the country. We also want to thank Maria Drees, our book coordinator, and Pete Feely, our manuscript and production editor, for their hard work bringing many different pieces together.

Introduction

The NCTE/IRA standards for the English language arts have three interrelated parts (see back cover): (1) the content standards themselves (NCTE/IRA, 1996); (2) descriptions of classroom practice in the *Standards Consensus* and the *Standards in Practice* series; and (3) performance standards, or the *Standards Exemplar Series*. This book is one of the three books in the *Standards Exemplar Series* and is intended for those who have wondered how teachers have translated NCTE's English language arts standards into student performance and how teachers have ranked that performance. This book will provide examples of both rankings of student work and translations of the English standards into student performances.

Two approaches are now used in the United States to describe content standards and performance standards—specification and principles/exemplification. In specification, content standards and levels of performance are described by small bits of behavior from one part of the language system. Usually these specifications are sequenced by grade level. The answers are right or wrong, and the sequence is certain. For example, one state has mandated in its content standards that "modifiers" be taught in the elementary grades, that pronoun case be taught in middle school, and that pronoun reference be taught in high school. Clearly, however, "modifiers" and the other parts of the language system are learned throughout the grades, not just in one. Another state wants the use of commas-in-a-series taught in one grade, and commas-for-nonrestrictive-clauses or phrases taught in another. These sequences never work in the classroom. Why? Many reasons. For one thing, one part of the language system influences others. For example, the use of particular phrase and clause modifiers produces new problems in punctuation.

Although specification will not work to produce a list of content standards, specification will work to identify parts of the performance standards assessing the content. Some knowledge in English language arts requires the specification of the names of things, and this kind of knowledge can be assessed with multiple-choice tests, which are good measures of most small-bit specifications. Most national and state programs use these multiple-choice tests and describe the performance levels at each grade level as a given number of right answers. These measures are useful for some purposes, but they have serious limits. We need more emphasis on principles in our descriptions of content standards and on exemplification in our descriptions of performance levels.

The approach used here to describe student performance levels is exemplification. Exemplification is used by the School Curriculum and Assessment Authority of Wales and England, by the National Assessment of Educational Progress (NAEP), by the College Board, and by some states, particularly California, Kentucky, and Vermont. Exemplification is not the same as specification, or the one-part-at-a-time/one-error-at-a-time approach. In specification, counting student "errors" produces judgments of quality, but counting errors alone is not an adequate measurement of quality in exemplification. In exemplification, instead of learning one part at a time, students learn one situation at a time in reading, writing, or speaking. Instead of measuring student achievement by adding up the number of right or wrong answers on a multiple-choice test, exemplification uses on-demand tasks and a range of portfolio entries to establish levels of student achievement. Exemplification then measures, with teacher judgments, the quality of performance in various situations. Exemplars show student performance on on-demand tasks in particular language situations, and portfolios show student performance on a range of tasks over time. All portfolio entries and tasks provide evidence of growth in achieving the content standards.

The On-Demand Tasks

Performance on each on-demand task is illustrated by an *exemplar* which is accompanied by a *rubric* describing features, a *commentary* describing connections between rubrics and exemplars, and an index of how each task is connected to the content standards. An *exemplar* is a sample of a student performance on a task in a given situation (i.e., a situation sample), accompanied by a *rubric* and a *commentary* on that sample. Thus, in this book, levels of performance are described with (1) a description of an on-demand task, which represents one or more of the principles in the content standards and which has been tried out in many classrooms; (2) grade-level *exemplars* of student work on specific on-demand tasks requiring particular kinds of knowledge in English language arts (e.g., writing reports, responding to literature); (3) *rubrics* describing the different achievement levels for a given task and situation; and (4) *commentaries* showing the relationship of each sample to the rubric. In general, three achievement levels—high, middle, and low—are presented for each on-demand task. The achievement levels make visible the values and standards that teachers share. On-demand tasks sometimes are used only for assessment. Sometimes they are used only for classroom instruction. Sometimes for both.

The Portfolio Tasks

A portfolio is a collection over time of student performances on classroom assignments. These assignments are tasks showing the student's performance in a range of knowledge domains in English language arts, the student's development throughout the year, and the processes used by students in various tasks—all based on the content standards. This book presents three portfolios which exemplify achievement on the standards. Each has been ranked at one of three achievement levels: high, middle, or low. For each entry in the portfolio, marginal comments based on a rubric will highlight strengths and weaknesses of that particular piece. Following each portfolio is a summary commentary which links the portfolio as a whole to the rubrics and marginal comments.

The Rubrics

The rubrics that accompany the student samples in this book are drawn from several rubrics and frameworks for assessing student performances in English language arts. The only requirement was that these rubrics and frameworks be consistent with the NCTE/IRA content standards. Rubrics usually focus on particular kinds of writing or particular purposes and audiences, giving general descriptors of several levels of performance. In the *Exemplar Series,* the introduction describes the content standards as kinds of knowledge and activities, and the rubrics are situation-specific and achievement-level-specific.

The Commentaries

In exemplification, a description of an achievement level must have three parts—samples or exemplars of performance, rubric, and commentary. All three are necessary. The commentary describes the links between rubrics and samples, pointing to specific evidence from the sample and adding evaluations of the overall work.

Connections to Standards

On-demand tasks and items in the portfolios are indexed to one or more of the NCTE/IRA standards. For each task, target standards are those directly met by the assignment. Supplementary standards are those which are met when the task is embedded in a larger instructional unit. Instruction always involves many standards at any one time.

STANDARDS IN THE CLASSROOM

Standards for the English Language Arts (SELA) tells us that in the classroom we will find (1) students who are playing the roles of readers and writers, discovering how to shape their experience and to connect their experience to text; (2) evidence of public audiences, classroom audiences, and personal audiences playing the roles of reader and responder to student work; (3) subject matter, whether imaginary, public/civic, or academic and informational; (4) different tools (computers, telephones, calculators, faxes) and editing groups; (5) various texts both literary and nonliterary for reading, hearing, and viewing; (6) language reference books on the structure of grammar (phonology, morphology, syntax) and text; and (7) evidence of cognitive and metacognitive development in drafts from editing, discussion, and response groups, including learning logs, outlines, notes, and other forms. The content and processes of the classroom include *reading, writing, speaking, listening, viewing,* and *representing.* On a map, the classroom might look like this:

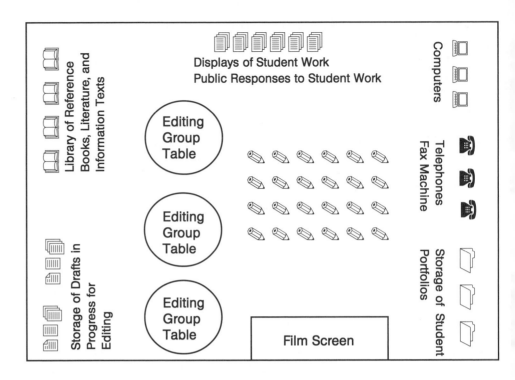

From the student work in this typical classroom, teachers have specified some kinds of performance as particularly salient: (1) narrative writing (writing firsthand reports, autobiography, and biography), (2) argumentative writing (editorials, problem solutions, letters to the editor, position statements), (3) report writing (newspaper reports, portraits, information summaries), (4) reading depth—response to literature (character analysis, intertextual comparisons, short story evaluations, summaries), (5) reading depth—response to informational texts (history, general information, bus schedules), (6) reading breadth (reading journals, book logs), and (7) visual representation, including mapping and charts. These are not the only performances of importance, but they are common performances in English classes and are stressed in *Standards for the English Language Arts*. Each of the three books in this exemplar series (K–5, 6–8, 9–12) includes most of these types, but not necessarily all. Speaking, listening, and viewing rarely appear. But they are an important part of the content standards.

A FRAMEWORK FOR ASSESSMENT

What do exemplars of on-demand tasks and portfolios tell us about what students know? Exemplars of on-demand tasks and portfolios exhibit the standards in action in *three ways of knowing,* in *six activities or forms of representation,* in *four domains of knowledge* in English language arts, and in *various patterns of student development.*

Three Ways of Knowing

The three ways of knowing are, first, declarative or content knowledge ("knowing that"), including the knowledge usually exhibited by students in traditional multiple-choice tests ("The main character is a spider"); second, procedural or process knowledge ("knowing how"), including the use of reading strategies, writing strategies, and strategies for turning various kinds of knowledge into action; and third, background or general awareness knowledge, including general awareness of the purposes of language ("knowing about/why").

    I. *Knowing that* is the factual, informational knowledge of English language arts, including information about genre, literary forms, and rules of spelling or punctuation or subject-verb agreement (see the four domains of knowledge below). *Knowing that* is developed through use, memorization, and multiple readings. *Knowing that* can often be assessed with multiple-choice tests, but this approach alone is inadequate. Constructed responses reveal how well students can contextualize information.

II. *Knowing how* is the procedural or process knowledge of action, of using the four domains of knowledge in an actual situation. One can name the parts of a sentence (*knowing that*) and still not be able to write one (*knowing how*). *Knowing how* requires assessment during the use of language. Six uses are emphasized here: reading, writing, speaking, listening, viewing, and representing (see activities below).

III. *Knowing about* is a general awareness of language structure and use. *Knowing about* requires a broad awareness of contexts for language use and experiences with many situations requiring variations in language use. *Knowing about* is developed through broad exploration and choice and is assessed in both multiple-choice tests and constructed responses.

These three ways of knowing—knowing that, knowing how, and knowing about—shape the breadth and depth of knowledge from the four domains of English language arts—cognition, rhetoric, linguistics/conventions, and cultural themes or ideas from the humanities. (See Figure 1, p. xviii.) These three ways of knowing and four domains of knowledge interact in the six activities of English language arts.

Six Activities or Forms of Representation

The six activities or forms of representation of English language arts are reading, writing, speaking, listening, viewing, and representing. Students who prepare graphics for a speech or a filmed drama are engaged in representing in English. Viewing refers to the knowledge needed to comprehend a graphic (e.g., a bus schedule), an illustration, or a filmed drama.

Four Domains of Knowledge

I. *Cognition* involves three kinds of cognitive processes. Two are strategies:

- strategies for fluent processing in basic decoding (refers to learning the code in reading) and encoding (refers to learning the code in writing);

- strategies for metacognitive processing (thinking about thinking), including processes for initial understanding, putting ideas together (interpretation), connecting personal experience and text, summarizing and paraphrasing, and developing a critical stance. The chart below, developed by Brian White (1995) using perspectives, strategies, and explanations from Beach and Marshall (1991), illustrates different cognitive processes at work:

Basic Perspectives	Response Strategies	Explanations of Response Strategies
Textual	Describing	"Readers describe a text when they restate or reproduce information that is provided verbatim in the text" (p. 29).
Textual	Conceiving	"When readers conceive of characters, settings, and language, they are moving beyond the description of information in order to make statements about its meaning" (p. 29).
Textual	Interpreting	"Interpreting a text involves defining the symbolic meaning, theme, or point of specific events in the text. In making interpretations, we are usually discussing what the text 'says' " (p. 143).
Textual	Close Reading	Students engaged in close reading focus on the structure of the text (rhyme scheme, meter, organization) and other aspects of the text's surface.
Social	Engaging	When readers engage a text, they "articulate their emotional reaction or level of involvement. Such responses can take a variety of forms. 'This is BORING,' 'What a dumb story,' and 'I couldn't put it down' " are typical responses (p. 28).

Social	Connecting	"It is when readers 'connect' their own experience to the materials in the text that the interactions between reader and text become most evident. The characters or situations in a story may remind us of autobiographical events or of characters and situations in other texts" (p. 31).
Topical	Explaining	"Once we have constructed a tentative conception of characters' behavior, we must still explain as best we can why those characters are behaving as they are" (p. 30). Our explanations derive from our knowledge of social, psychological, and political forces operating on characters, and our knowledge of "topics" such as alcoholism, maturation, courtship, urban life.
Cultural	Judging	"When we pull away from a text . . . we make judgments about the characters in the story or about the literary quality of the text as a whole" (p. 33). Such judgments, as Scholes (1985) has argued, are based upon socially and culturally derived criteria.

- the third cognitive process involves <u>habits-of-mind</u>: a tolerance of ambiguity, of the need to review and reread, of uncertainty, of the need to take risks in one's estimates and guesses.

II. *Rhetoric* refers to interactions among narrator, audience, subject, and types of discourse (literary, information):

- <u>distance of narrator to an audience</u> (Is the audience close or distant?): In English, students learn such things as how to shift in their writing from close, conversational audiences to the distant, formal audiences of public discourse;

- <u>distance of narrator to a subject</u> (Is the subject personal or impersonal?): In English, students learn in their reading such things as how to distinguish between narrators who are in the past or present, here or there, participants or observers, and narrators who are providing information or interpretations;

- <u>narrator perspective</u>: in English, students learn different perspectives— telling and showing, reliable and unreliable narrators, serious and comic, indirect (ironical) and direct, formal and informal;

- <u>reader stance</u>: in English, students learn to shift from the poetic (literary) to the transactional (information) stance in their reading and writing.

III. *Linguistics/Conventions* refers to three kinds of language structures and practices:

- <u>text structures:</u> paragraphs, meter, rhyme, figures of speech, literary forms, and so forth. For example, in English, students learn things about the structure of narratives, descriptions, arguments, etc.;

- <u>language structure (grammar):</u> in English, students learn about phonology (sound), morphology (words), syntax (phrases and sentences);

- <u>conventions (mechanics):</u> in English, students learn about spelling, punctuation, usage, capitalization, other editing forms. Each school site needs a style or convention guide to help teachers and students focus on conventions of special significance. It is clear that students learn to read and to write by reading and writing; sometimes, students need to isolate parts of the language. Students are often tested on some combination of these three kinds of knowledge about language. For example, the National Assessment of Educational Progress used the following analysis of language structure and conventions to analyze student writing (Applebee, Langer, and Mullis, 1987):

A. Sentence Types

1. Simple—A sentence that contains a subject and a verb. It may also have an object, subject complement, phrase, nominative absolute, or verbal. Also a word group used in dialogue, for emphasis, or as an exclamation that is not an independent clause.

2. Compound—A sentence containing two or more simple sentences joined by something other than a comma.

3. Complex (and compound-complex)—A sentence that contains at least one independent clause and one dependent clause.

4. Run-on

   a. Fused—A sentence containing two or more independent clauses with no punctuation or conjunction separating them.

   b. On and on—A sentence consisting of four or more independent clauses strung together with conjunctions.

   c. Comma splice—A sentence containing two or more independent clauses separated by a comma instead of a semicolon or a coordinating conjunction.

5. Fragment—A word group, other than an independent clause, written and punctuated as a sentence.

B. Faulty Sentence Construction

1. Agreement Error—A sentence in which at least one of the following occurs: subject and verb do not agree, pronoun and antecedent do not agree, noun and modifier do not agree, subject/object pronoun is misused, or verb tense shifts.

2. Awkward Sentence

   a. Faulty parallelism—A parallel construction that is semantically or structurally dysfunctional.

   b. Unclear pronoun reference—A pronoun's antecedent is unclear.

   c. Illogical construction—Faulty modification or a dangling modifier or a functionally misarranged or misproportioned sentence.

   d. Other dysfunctions—A sentence containing an omitted or extra word or a split construction that definitely detracts from readability.

C. Punctuation Errors

Errors of commission and errors of omission in the use of commas, dashes, quotation marks, semicolons, apostrophes, and end marks.

D. Problems in Word-Level Conventions

1. Word Choice—The writer needs a word that is different from the one written. This category also includes attempts at a verb, adjective, or adverb form that is nonexistent or unacceptable.

2. Spelling—In addition to a misspelling, this category includes word-division errors at the end of a line, two words written as one, one word written as two, superfluous plurals, and groups of distinguishable letters that do not make a legitimate word.

3. Capitalization—The first word in a sentence is not capitalized, a proper noun or adjective within a sentence is not capitalized, or the pronoun "I" is not capitalized.

IV. *Cultural Themes or Ideas* comprise three kinds of concepts from the humanities:

• core concepts like the ideas of historical periods, the hero, coming of age, setting, character, and ethics, among others. These core concepts are part of the central narratives of English language arts;

• dual concepts like stance (poetic and transactional), multiculturalism or pluralism (difference and commonality), choice (freedom and fate), foreshadowing (ambiguity and predictability), community (individual and society), and organization (rational and intuitive), among others;

• metaphorical concepts that structure the narratives of English language arts (e.g., the world as a machine with part-whole relationships, life as an organism with growth over time, knowledge as a mirror or lamp, democracy as a search for common bonds).

A word needs to be said about the materials or texts focusing on the ideas of an English class. Remember that cognition, rhetoric (different audiences), and linguistics/ conventions (text and conventions) are the other three domains of knowledge in English language arts, and we have grammar books, composition texts, and strategy lists to help us think about those domains. But what books and materials help us think about the ideas of English language arts? English teachers across the country attempt to answer this question when they select the literature they will purchase for a given grade level.

Advanced Placement teachers, who focus on the last two years of high school, have selected the following authors as, among other things, helpful writers about the key ideas of English language arts in high schools:

Poetry

W. H. Auden; Elizabeth Bishop; William Blake; Anne Bradstreet; E. K. Brathwaite; Gwendolyn Brooks; Robert Browning; Lord Byron; Samuel Taylor Coleridge; H. D.; Emily Dickinson; John Donne; T. S. Eliot; Robert Frost; George Herbert; Gerard Manley Hopkins; Langston Hughes; Ben Jonson; John Keats; Philip Larkin; Robert Lowell; Andrew Marvell; John Milton; Marianne Moore; Sylvia Plath; Alexander Pope; Adrienne Rich; William Shakespeare; Percy Bysshe Shelley; Alfred Lord Tennyson; Walt Whitman; Richard Wilbur; William Carlos Williams; William Wordsworth; William Butler Yeats

Drama

Edward Albee; Samuel Beckett; William Congreve; Oliver Goldsmith; Lorraine Hansberry; Lillian Hellman; Ben Jonson; Arthur Miller; Sean O'Casey; Eugene O'Neill; Harold Pinter; William Shakespeare; George Bernard Shaw; Richard Brinsley Sheridan; Tom Stoppard; Oscar Wilde; Tennessee Williams; August Wilson

Prose Fiction (Novel and Short Story)

Chinua Achebe; Margaret Atwood; Jane Austen; James Baldwin; Saul Bellow; Emily and Charlotte Brontë; Willa Cather; John Cheever; Kate Chopin; Joseph Conrad; Stephen Crane; Charles Dickens; George Eliot; Ralph Ellison; Louise Erdrich; William Faulkner; Henry Fielding; F. Scott Fitzgerald; Ford Madox Ford; Thomas Hardy; Nathaniel Hawthorne; Ernest Hemingway; Zora Neale Hurston; Henry James; James Joyce; D. H. Lawrence; Bernard Malamud; Katherine Mansfield; Carson McCullers; Herman Melville; Toni Morrison; Vladimir Nabokov; Flannery O'Connor; Cynthia Ozick; Katherine Anne Porter; Jean Rhys; Jonathan Swift; Mark Twain; John Updike; Alice Walker; Eudora Welty; Edith Wharton; Virginia Woolf; Richard Wright

Expository Literature

Joseph Addison; Matthew Arnold; James Baldwin; James Boswell; Thomas Carlyle; Ralph Waldo Emerson; William Hazlitt; Samuel Johnson; Charles Lamb; Norman Mailer; Mary McCarthy; H. L. Mencken; John Stuart Mill; George Orwell; Richard Steele; Lewis Thomas; Henry David Thoreau; Barbara Tuchman; Virginia Woolf

(From *Advanced Placement Course Description Booklets,* English, May 1993, The College Board, pages 38, 39.)

Teachers report that the eleven most frequently required authors in grades 9 through 12 are Shakespeare, Steinbeck, Dickens, Twain, Miller, Orwell, Lee, Hawthorne, Hemingway, Fitzgerald, and Golding, and by grade level, the three most popular titles are:

Grade 9: *Romeo and Juliet, Great Expectations, To Kill a Mockingbird*
Grade 10: *Julius Caesar, The Pearl, To Kill a Mockingbird*
Grade 11: *The Scarlet Letter, The Adventures of Huckleberry Finn, The Great Gatsby*
Grade 12: *Hamlet, Macbeth, Lord of the Flies, 1984*

(Information above from Arthur Applebee, *A Study of Book-Length Works Taught in High School English Courses,* 1989, Center for the Learning and Teaching of Literature, University at Albany, SUNY.)

Other selections which appear frequently on high school lists are: *The Color Purple* (Walker), *Animal Farm* (Orwell), *The Call of the Wild* (London), *Things Fall Apart* (Achebe), *Brave New World* (Huxley), *The House on Mango Street* (Cisneros), *Nectar in a Sieve* (Markandaya), *The Diary of a Young Girl* (Frank), *Of Mice and Men* (Steinbeck), *A*

Separate Peace (Knowles), *Woman Warrior* (Kingston), *Native Son* (Wright), *Journey to Topaz* (Uchida), *Song of Solomon* (Morrison), *Their Eyes Were Watching God* (Hurston), *I Know Why the Caged Bird Sings* (Angelou), *Cry the Beloved Country* (Paton), *In Our Time* (Hemingway), *Roll of Thunder, Hear My Cry* (Taylor), *Wuthering Heights* (Brontë), *The Red Badge of Courage* (Crane), *A Raisin in the Sun* (Hansberry), *The Old Man and the Sea* (Hemingway), *Heart of Darkness* (Conrad), *The Joy Luck Club* (Tan), *All Quiet on the Western Front* (Remarque), *Cyrano de Bergerac* (Rostand), *The Crucible* (Miller), *The Glass Menagerie* (Williams), *Oedipus Rex* (Sophocles), *Antigone* (Sophocles), *Death of a Salesman* (Miller), *The Miracle Worker* (Gibson), *Othello* (Shakespeare), and *Our Town* (Wilder).

These lists and others like them are intended to help teachers at the local level generate their own discussion about what books might be selected. The central point is that English classes read and describe narratives about our common humanity, our border crossings, our building of a democratic community, in the midst of our fears and our inevitable mistakes. Within these narratives, we find a body of core concepts, informing metaphors, and dualisms.

Patterns of Development

The framework on the inside back cover shows the interaction of the three ways of knowing and the four domains. The rubrics and commentaries are based on this framework. A given student performance—say, writing an editorial about a controversial issue—will often include all four domains and the three ways of knowing. The rubrics and commentaries will show how these domains and ways of knowing are reflected in exemplars of performance from both on-demand tasks and portfolios. In addition, the rubrics and commentaries will consider the developmental patterns that influence the four domains and the three ways of knowing. A developmental pattern is shaped by a student's prior knowledge, by interests at a particular time in life, and by a student's range of support and help. A student who does not receive particular kinds of help at a particular time may not achieve at a high level.

In this book, the four domains of knowledge (cognition, rhetoric, linguistics/conventions, themes/ideas) are represented in the rubrics and commentaries as four kinds of developmental tensions. For example:

I. Cognition:

A. Slow Decoding/Encoding   vs.   Fluent Processing
Fragmented   *Automatic*

Example: In development, the writer's scrawl can, with interaction and help, slowly develop into alphabetic writing.

B. No Metacognition   vs.   Metacognition: Thinking about Thinking
Extensive scaffolding (help) by others   *Selected scaffolding (help) by others*
Fragmented tool use   *Internal self-scaffolding and control of tools*

Example: In development, the writer or reader may begin with extensive assistance and move to more fully internalized habits of reflection on thinking.

C. Memory   vs.   Reason and Reflection
Learning by memory only   *Learning by memory and reason/reflection*

Example: In development, the writer or reader may begin with copying and memorizing and later add interpreting and critiquing.

II. Rhetoric:

A. Reader/Writer as Audience   vs.   External Communities as Audience
Close/personal   *Far/impersonal*

B. Reader/Writer as Subject   vs.   External World as Subject
Close/personal   *Far/impersonal*
Expressive subject   *Detached ("objective")*

Example: In development, the writer often begins with close, personal audiences and subjects and moves toward more flexibility in writing—to different audiences and on different subjects.

C. Direct Perspective   vs.   Indirect Perspective
Irony/comedy

Example: In development, the writer or reader appears to begin with a direct perspective and later adds the indirect perspectives of comedy, irony, and others.

III. Linguistics/Conventions:

A. Language/Text   vs.   Analytic Features/Paradigmatic Structures
Synthetic/narrative case structures

Example: In development, the student often begins with narrative structures and moves toward some use of analytical forms as well.

B. Small Forms   vs.   Larger Forms

Example: In development, the writer or reader often begins with knowledge about small forms (sounds, letters, words, simple sentences) and later adds elaborated sentences and elaborated stories.

IV. Themes or Ideas:

A. Ideas/Themes   vs.
    Folk/everyday   *Scientific/academic*
    Ideas/concepts   *Concepts*
    Estimations   *Definitions*

Example: In development, the writer often moves from everyday forms of knowledge to an understanding of academic forms of knowledge as well.

These are not the only developmental patterns which teachers have identified in the work of students at different ages. But these patterns illustrate some of the variations teachers attend to when they are trying to estimate growth in the English language arts. In writing and responding to literature, for example, the student is often experiencing the tensions between the personal response, which connects the text to one's internal experiences or one's values, and the analytical response, which connects the text to other texts and to ideas from the external world. The student may also be experiencing the tension between a case (for example, an autobiography) and a more generalized exposition (a larger intertextual pattern involving several cases). The student may also be trying to tell the narrative of boundary crossings, experiencing the tensions between tradition or the new and the past or present (e.g., placing Huck Finn in a contemporary problem or issue). In each instance, these tensions are part of a developmental pattern which influences the student's performance. Some of the other tensions of developmental patterns are suggested in Figure 2 on p. xix.

CONNECTIONS TO STANDARDS

The four domains of knowledge in English language arts are described in many places in *Standards for the English Language Arts*. For example:

1. *Cognition* is described in Standards 3, 5, and 10. For example: "if [students] are reading something that is especially challenging or foreign to them, they may need to pause frequently to search for graphic, phonological, syntactic, and semantic clues that will help them make sense of the text" (page 32).

2. *Rhetoric* is described in Standards 4, 7, and 12. For example: "Even handwriting can reflect a consideration of audience: scribbles may work when writing personal notes; however, directions to others on how to get to an unknown destination will most likely require clear and complete writing" (page 34).

3. *Linguistics/conventions* are described in Standards 6, 9, and 11. For example: "students need a working knowledge of the systems and structures of language as well as familiarity with accepted language conventions, including grammar, punctuation, spelling, and the formal elements of visual texts" (page 36).

4. *Themes or ideas* are described in Standards 1, 2, and 8. For example: Literary works "give students opportunities to engage in ethical and philosophical reflection on the values and beliefs of their own cultures, of other cultures, and of other times and places" (page 30).

The six activities or forms of representation are also described in the Standards:

1. *Reading:* Standards 1, 2, and 3 describe the content and processes of reading.

2. *Writing:* Standards 4, 5, and 6 describe the content and processes of writing.

3. *Speaking:* Standards 4 and 12 describe the emphasis on speaking.

4. *Listening:* Standards 7, 8, and 9 emphasize the importance of listening.

5. *Viewing:* Standard 3 introduces the importance of comprehending and interpreting graphics, and high school vignette 5 describes the importance of film study.

6. *Representing:* Standard 4 introduces visual language, and middle school vignette 2 provides an example of mapping.

The standards also call for all three ways of knowing—knowing that, knowing how, and knowing about. To match standards and assessments, teachers are urged to review *Standards for the English Language Arts* carefully.

Each section of this book contains descriptions of how various on-demand tasks and portfolio entries represent achievement of the English standards. Because this book presents samples of students responding to challenges representing one or more of the standards for the English language arts, you can use this book to illustrate what the NCTE English standards might look like in practice. The student responses presented here are representative of high, middle, and low achievement levels within a limited sample, but these student responses are not necessarily the full range of student responses. Furthermore, many parts of the standards for the English language arts are not represented here. For example, discussion, dramatic activities, and performance on multiple-choice tests are not included. Nevertheless, the samples contained in this book should help you paint a portrait of some of your goals in the English language arts.

In the design of the book, we have made it easy to see how the on-demand tasks and portfolios illustrate the NCTE/IRA English standards. Open up the first flap of the back cover and notice that the standards are on your right, and the samples are on your left. Of course, the list of standards included here is not a substitute for their full explanation and discussion in *Standards for the English Language Arts,* to which we refer you, but it can help you in mapping standards to exemplars. Teachers at NCTE's 1996 Spring Conference in Boston, for example, tried mapping NCTE/IRA standards to particular student performances, and those teachers found, as you will find, that the exemplars often incorporate many standards. In addition, you can use the other two books in the *Standards Exemplar Series* (for grades K–5 and 6–8) to see how the exemplars for particular standards change across the grades. By looking through all three exemplar books, you will find that in general students at particular ages do better on some tasks.

If you open out the standards page, you will see a framework for assessing student performance in the English language arts. This framework is explained in detail on pages x–xvi of this introduction. As you study and discuss the exemplars and portfolios, you can use the framework to generate your own descriptive statements about what a particular piece of student work shows about what a student knows and can do. The framework on the inside back flap contains some sample "starter" statements. On the innermost side of the back cover is a chart cross-referencing the on-demand tasks and the portfolio pieces. You can use this chart to locate additional examples of particular kinds of performances (e.g., reports of information) and to identify differences and similarities between on-demand tasks and portfolio pieces. The list of various kinds of performances in on-demand tasks and portfolios appears in the table of contents.

Finally, you should use this book to start discussions with students, with fellow teachers, and with parents about achievement levels in the range and the depth of understanding English and the English language arts. In portfolios showing several items from one student, you will find that a poor performance on one or two tasks does not necessarily represent what a student potentially can do, and by looking at a collection of tasks from one student, you will find out something about the student's range of skills in the English language arts. We urge you to share the student samples with your students and to ask your students to rank the samples, to write comments explaining their rankings, and then to share this information with other students. We recommend that teachers order a class set of the series in order to illustrate for students what portfolios look like and what various assignments look like. We also suggest that you ask parents to rank samples and discuss their rankings together. We recommend that you do the same with fellow teachers. Try scoring the student samples yourself, alone or with others, and then compare your rankings with those in the book. The rankings, the commentaries, and the rubrics come from many places across the country and have been tried out in many places, but that does not mean that your local ranking might not involve an insight into a work which the others missed. We will reserve space on NCTE's Web site for an electronic discussion of your responses (http://www.ncte.org).

Figure 1 shows another way of thinking about the three types of knowledge. That is, taken together, knowing that, knowing how, and knowing about may be viewed as constituting breadth and depth in reading, writing, speaking, listening, viewing, and representing.

Figure 1: Sample Performances for Assessing Breadth and Depth in the English Language Arts

The Three Types of Knowledge in the Six Activities	The Four Domains of Knowledge in the English Language Arts			
	Cognition: Processing	Rhetoric: Distancing	Linguistics/Conventions: Grammar Structures, Text Structures, and Conventions	Themes/Ideas: Constructing
Reading: Breadth and Depth (knowing that, knowing how, and knowing about)	Shows fluency in reading; Makes correct guesses about thoughts of characters	Depth: Reads in depth—first-person narrator; Breadth: Reads a range of narrators	Reads a range of forms—poems, novels, short stories, magazines, newspapers	Traces a single idea in history; Reads a range of opinions by different authors on same issue
Writing: Breadth and Depth (knowing that, knowing how, and knowing about)	Shows automaticity in handwriting; Drafts of argument show strategies of questioning, believing, disbelieving, summarizing, clarifying; Shows evidence of editing conventions	Shows ability to shift point of view of work—from first to second person; Writes to three different audiences on public issue	Shows ability to write in different literary forms—poems, short stories—and in different nonliterary forms—reports, editorials, letters, features	Shows sense of theme, place, and character in writing of literary text
Breadth and Depth in *Speaking and Listening* (knowing that, knowing how, and knowing about)	Shows fluency in speaking; Drafts show use of multiple sources in development of speech	Leads small-group discussion and then reports or listens to large group in large-group discussion	Uses diverse structures in speech, from narrative to exposition and argument	Gives speech to class on public issue
Viewing: Breadth and Depth (knowing that, knowing how, and knowing about)	Shows fluency in reading graphs; Makes correct location of bus times	Can redo line graph as bar graph	Understands flashback device in film	Can summarize plot of film
Representing: Breadth and Depth (knowing that, knowing how, and knowing about)	Can organize portfolio in some kind of sequence		Can produce a clear table of contents	Can organize book log by theme

These three kinds of knowledge from four different domains develop in different ways throughout the grades. Therefore, the performance of students will show some typical developmental patterns which are reflected in the samples, rubrics, and commentaries. These developmental patterns are presented in Figure 2.

Figure 2: Typical Patterns of Development in Domains of English Language Arts

		The Four Domains of Knowledge in the English Language Arts						
		Cognition: Processing		Rhetoric: Distancing		Linguistics/Conventions: Grammar Structures, Text Structures, and Conventions		Themes/Ideas: Constructing
		Encoding/ Decoding	Processing and Metacognitive Strategies	Distance from Audience	Distance from Subject	Text Structure	Grammar Modeling	Core Concepts / Dual Concepts
Some Typical Developmental Patterns		From experience to mapping/ drawing to print code	From recording to reporting to generalizing	From first-person experience to third-person reflections		Grammar: from sound to word to phrase		From the sense of an idea to the structure of an idea
		From garbles and fragments to conventions and fluency	From processing procedures to thinking about thinking	From expressive audience (self) to distant public audiences		Text: from narrative to paradigmatic modes Grammar: from additive to embedded structures Conventions: from letter (print) to sounds; from word (spelling) to phrase (commas)		From everyday concepts like "the hero" to scientific/academic concepts like "the psychology of leadership"
		From need for much assistance to selected scaffolding						

REFERENCES

Applebee, A. N. (April 1989). *A study of book-length works taught in high school English courses.* Report Series 1.2. Albany: State University of New York at Albany, Center for the Learning and Teaching of Literature. ERIC #ED309453.

Applebee, A. N., Langer, J., & Mullis, I. V. S. (1987). *Grammar, punctuation, and spelling: Controlling the conventions of written English at ages 9, 13, and 17.* NAEP Report No. 15–W03. Princeton, NJ: Educational Testing Service.

Beach, R., and Marshall, J. (1991). *Teaching literature in the secondary school.* New York: Harcourt Brace Jovanovich.

College Board, The. (May 1993). *Advanced placement course description booklets.* English. New York: The College Board.

Scholes, R. *Textual power: Literary theory and the teaching of English.* New Haven, CT: Yale University Press.

White, B. (1995). Assuming nothing: A pre-methods diagnostic in the teaching of literature. *English Education 27*(4), 221–239.

Exemplars

This section contains exemplars of performances commonly expected of high school students. Each exemplar consists of a description of an on-demand task, a sample of student performance, a rubric describing the achievement level of that performance, and a commentary showing the relationship of the performance to the rubric. In most cases, the exemplars appear in sets which illustrate high, middle, and low levels of performance on a common task.

At the end of each set of exemplars is a graphic ("Connections to Standards") showing which of the standards for the English language arts are targeted by a particular performance in an on-demand setting. The second line of the graphic suggests additional standards that might be illustrated if the task were extended or embedded in a larger unit of classroom instruction.

Several of the exemplars in this section were selected from materials developed and published by the California Department of Education. For a number of years, the innovative assessments of writing and reading developed by California educators have provided models and inspiration for a variety of national, state, district, and school-level assessment projects. Thousands of California educators and their students participated in the development, field testing, revising, benchmarking, and scoring of the samples shown here. The exemplars selected from California's writing and reading assessments have been slightly altered from their original format. Specifically, the rubrics which accompany the work samples have been adapted to reflect the framework presented in the introduction (pp. x–xvi) of this book and on its inside back cover. Second, in the California assessments, student work received one or more numerical scores, ranging from 0 to 6. Numerical scores do not appear in this book: performances are described as being in the high, middle, or low range.

Several other exemplars were selected from materials developed and published by the College Board. These tasks were administered to students in grades 9–12 in junior high and high schools from Maine to Oregon. The teachers who worked on the College Board tasks used numerical scores which have been translated here into high, middle, and low range performances. In addition, rubrics and commentaries have been adapted to reflect the framework of this book.

NARRATIVE (AUTOBIOGRAPHY)

Task

To assess the student's capacity to compose from personal experience, the teacher asks students to write various forms of autobiography. In this task, the writer is asked to describe an incident from personal experience which includes, if possible, dialogue, movement or gestures, names of people or objects, and sensory details. The writer is asked to describe remembered feelings, understandings, or reflections at the time of the incident, and also, if possible, to evaluate the incident from his or her present perspective, implying or stating its significance to his or her life. In this narrative task, the student is asked to present a past event as if it were happening in front of the reader, either presenting the past as present or taking the reader into the past. In autobiography, the main character is the narrator.

Exemplar — High

Rubric

Cognition: Drafts of this paper might help trace the writer's effort to construct dialogue at key moments and to add details to elaborate particular moments. The drafts of the paper are needed to estimate many of the cognitive strategies used by the writer.

Rhetoric: The writer successfully attempts a difficult opening sentence, putting the reader directly into the narrative and putting the narrator at the center of the story.

Linguistics/Conventions: The writer handles some difficult sections very well. There are a few minor lapses in spelling and punctuation, but overall this first draft demonstrates excellent control of language structure and conventions.

Themes/Ideas: At the end, the writer evaluates the impact of the event on his or her view of self.

"GEEZE, it's hot today" I said to my friend Shawn "Thanks for inviting me to go swiming with you and your family."

"No problem" he replied. "I love taking my friend's to lurrtle lake; it's great for swiming and fishing.

"You want to swim to the other side"

"Shure"

Shawn and I waded into the lake. The water felt great, like a cool silky sheild protecting me from the sun. My shoulders slipped below the surface and I instantly felt refreshed. I started to kick and was soon crusing across the surface at a leasurly speed, taking the time to roll over on my back and relax here and there.

Shawn was starting to fall behind so I stopped to tread water and wait for him. I noticed we were pretty far out and the water was pretty deep. All of a sudden I herd Shawn calling for help. I looked over and noticed that for some reason he couldn't stay afloat. I thought to myself "Oh God, he's drowning. I immedatly started swiming twords him. I had about ten yards to go when I realized "I didn't know what to do. I'd never been trained in rescuing drowning swimmers before. The one thing I did know was not to swim to them because they grab on to you so you can't swim either — which is exactly what he did once I got there. He had a grip like he was trying to give me a giant "bear hug," and proceeded to drag me under also. I paniced, my reflexes took over, and I broke his hold. His head immedatly went under I felt so helpless. Here we were out in the middle of this lake, no ones around except for the people on shore (who were too far away to here us call for help).

I — had no choice, I was Shawn's only hope; against every instict in my body, I reached out and grabbed him again. This time I was carefull, and made shure I grabed under his shoulde so he couldn't grab me.

Amazingly I managed to drag him all the way back to shore. Don't ask me how, because I don't remember. All I do remember, is the great feeling I got once it was all over. I was very proud of myself, for I had acted under pressure, and saved a friend's life. Oh, what a feeling!

Commentary

This writer puts the reader directly into the narrative from the first sentence. Most young writers are not willing to take this kind of risk, fearing that the audience will need every possible detail of the introductory material before entering the story. In this narrative, the writer gives the audience necessary background information as the story moves along. At one key moment, the writer stops to describe what he or she recalls about people who are drowning ("they grab on to you"). In the opening dialogue, several key pieces of information are embedded in on-going events (hot days, swimming invitation).

The writer also paces the story very effectively. After the opening dialogue, the story enters a slow period ("leisurely speed"), then a refreshing stage ("a cool silky sheild") in which the writer takes time to "relax here and there." Then tension enters the scene as Shawn falls behind the narrator when they are "pretty far out."

The writer shows a keen sense of how to organize the drama of the narrative, including using the dash twice to add dramatic tension at key moments, once after "they grab on to you so you can't swim either" and again between "I" and "had" in "I—had no choice."

Finally the narrative moves swiftly from "I felt so helpless" to "I managed to drag him." The writer leaves us with the suggestion that something within us takes over during a crisis, leaving us unable to know or remember all of the details but embedding within us a sense of our capacity to act under pressure. To convey this sense of the unknown and unremembered, the writer turns to those readers who want more details and says, "Don't ask me how" and closes with "Oh what a feeling." This paper is an outstanding narrative.

Exemplar

Middle

R u b r i c

Cognition: The writer needs to expand his or her editing strategies. Having someone else read the paper aloud would probably help.

Rhetoric: The writer has a good sense of what the audience needs to know to sustain interest in the drama of the narrative.

Linguistics/Conventions: A few spelling problems, run-on sentences, missing commas, and missing words weaken what is otherwise a well-written narrative.

Themes/Ideas: The writer does not evaluate the significance of the incident, beyond commenting about how he or she felt about the incident overall.

Commentary

The writer quietly builds the tension, beginning with the pitcher's collapse in the last inning and the writer's role as the only pitcher left. The writer describes the moment entering the game with simple, telling details: "I wasn't nervous and everything was quiet." The next hitter is quickly described and then we move to the central incident, the hitter up with two outs and bases loaded. Here, the writer stops the action in order to let us know more about the past exploits of this particular hitter. Then we move quickly through the next two pitches, both foul balls (strikes), and then the action stops again. The writer focuses on the next and final pitch, telling us about practicing a curve ball in the backyard. Throughout the description, the writer attempts to give us the report without letting emotions show. Then at the end says, "I was so happy." This is a well-structured narrative, and with some editing could easily be a top paper.

My personal achievement came to in baseball We were playing in the championship game for our League. We had our best pitcher pitching and he wasn't doing to well It was the last inning of the game and he had walked the bases loaded with one out He had a bad temper and was mad at himself that's why he wasn't doing good. All of our other pitchers couldn't pitch that game except for me. I was a rookie that year but also pretty good. Our pitcher had a full count on the batter but if he walked him the game would be tied, so he took himself out of the game. I had to come in relief for him. I remember I wasn't that nervous and everything was quiet. The umpire told me that there was one out bases were loaded and I had a full count on the batter. If I walked him the game would be tied. I threw the pitch and he hit the ball right back at me and threw it home for one out. Now there were two outs and the bases were loaded. The next batter up was one the team's best hitters. Earlier in the year he hit a home-run off me so he was cocky when he got up there. The first two pitches I threw were strikes but he hit them about 300 ft foul. So I had no balls and two strikes, so I wanted a pitch so he wouldn't know what was coming next. I had experimented with my curve ball in the backyard with my dad before and pretty confident I could throw it for a strike. So I let it up and the batter had no idea it was coming. He swung and missed by about a foot. Then I heard all the voices again in the crowd cheering, and the next thing I know I was on the ground getting dog piled by my teamates. I was so happy. I had won the game for us I would temporally be a hero for my team.

Exemplar — Low

AN INCIDNT THAT SHOWED ME
AN IMPORTANT POINT IN MY LIFE
WAS HOW PEOPLE ALWAYS THINK
YOU ARE OUT TO DO BETTER
THEN THEM. SO THEY PUT
AN INVISIBLE CEILING OVER
YOUR GOAL IN LIFE. I WAS
KNOWLEGDABLE THIS IMPORTANT POINT
IN LIFE TRYING TO GET A
JOB THAT I CAN ACTUALLY
RECIEVE MONEY FROM AFTER TAKES,
GAS MONEY, AND FOOD
ITS PHYSICALLY IMPOSIBLE TO BREAK
THROUGH THIS INVISIBLE CIELING
THY PUT ON KIDS. UNLESS YOU
KNOW SOMEBODY OR HAVE A RELATIVE
WORKING FOR THIS BUSINESS AND IS
A HIGH ENOUGH POSITION TO HIRE YOU
I THINK THIS IS UNFAIR
TO YOUNG ADULTS AND SHOULD
BE EASIER TO GET A HIGH PAYING
JOB.

R u b r i c

Cognition: The writer needs some experiences in editing groups, learning to hear the audience's confusions and pleas for evidence. If the writer read the paper aloud to a group, one rewrite would probably greatly improve the quality of the paper.

Rhetoric: The writer tends to forget that a reader needs help to follow the argument.

Linguistics/Conventions: The language structure needs work. Awkward and incomplete phrases weaken the essay. Spelling problems require attention.

Themes/Ideas: The writer is engaged with the central idea of the essay but does not describe the autobiographical incident that must be at the center of the discussion.

Commentary

Although this essay is a poignant response to the prompt, no incident is mentioned. The paper vaguely refers to a job search without identifying a specific incident. The significance of the search is clear in the statement that it is "physically imposible to break through this invisible cieling thy put on kids." This student needs practice in moving from generalizations to specific incidents; clearly, there is an incident somewhere behind this lament. The student's diction and ability to handle sentences show promise. With direction and practice, the student will be able to learn how to tell the story that this essay only hints at.

Connections to Standards

	STANDARDS											
Targeted	1	2	3	4	5	6	7	8	9	10	11	12
Supplementary	1	2	3	4	5	6	7	8	9	10	11	12

This autobiographical-narrative task targets writing standards 4, 5, and 6. If this task were embedded into a larger unit of classroom instruction, the writing of autobiographical narratives might be accompanied by such activities as reading and responding to literary and nonliterary autobiographies (1, 2) and conducting research (7). Reading and responding to the autobiographies of others can help students develop an understanding of and respect for diversity (9). Students whose first language is not English might use their first language in composing an autobiographical narrative (e.g., choosing to use words from or write dialogue in their native language) (10). Students can use autobiographical narrative to accomplish their own purposes, such as exploring their own life histories or creating a text for a literary magazine (11, 12).

REPORT OF INFORMATION (DESCRIPTION)

Task

To assess the student's awareness of language variation, teachers often ask students to write linguistic portraits of particular people. In this kind of task, the students are asked to write a linguistic portrait of a favorite or memorable person, presenting detailed information about language variation. This topic requires that the student observe closely, select appropriate details about language use, summarize information, and find an effective organizational structure for a collection of descriptive details. This kind of task helps create an awareness of language use which the student can use in many language situations.

Rubric

Cognition: The writer is fluent and moves easily between generalities and concrete details. The paper suggests the writer used several preplanning strategies.

Rhetoric: The writer brings a somewhat distant subject close to the reader through specific, concrete details.

Linguistics/Conventions: The writer effectively uses a variety of sentence structures and punctuation devices. In addition, the paper reflects careful editing, despite a few minor errors. The organizational structure has a clear sequence, including help transition words.

Themes/Ideas: A controlling idea, well developed and focused, dominates the paper. The student has an awareness of the dimensions of language variation and the concepts of language study.

A Linguistic Portrait of Mrs. Newman

Everybody has his or her own personal style of speaking, but of all the people I've met, I find Mrs. Newman's language the most fascinating. Her vocabulary covers a vast range of formal and informal words, all the way from old-fashioned words like "ilk" to 90's terms such as "gansta rap." Both her spoken language and body language are full of emotion, and there are many more qualities, such as her suprasegmentals and correct grammar, that make Mrs. Newman's language intriguing and pleasant to listen to.

First, Mrs. Newman has a very diverse vocabulary. She is famous in her Latin classes for using "big complicated words," "nifty-sounding words," but also words that would be found in students' conversations. A few of her attention-grabbing big words include "objet d'art" and "juxtaposition," along with terms for different rhetorical devices such as "prolepsis," "chiasmus," and "synecdoche." She also uses "nifty-sounding" old-fashioned words in phrases such as "*hither* and *thither*" and "you and your *ilk*." Although she uses many of these impressive words, she is nevertheless not afraid to use the sort of language that would be found in typical students' conversations. This would include "gansta rap," "big time alliteration," and "(Neptune, the) big cheese." This wide gap between formal and informal words often makes her lectures humorous and interesting; in fact, I cannot remember any day where there wasn't at least one sentence she said that made people smile or laugh.

Another technical aspect that makes Mrs. Newman's language so different than others is her painfully correct grammar. She always obeys (and tells others to follow) little grammatical rules that almost nobody bothers with anymore, such as differentiating between "who" and "whom," "shall" and "will," and making sure nobody ever makes mistakes such as saying "very/most unique." Mrs. Newman's correct grammar, along with her diverse vocabulary, makes her appear to be a very well-educated person.

A third thing that makes Mrs. Newman's language interesting is her suprasegmentals. Usually, when talking in a normal conversation, she has a little stutter, for example, "It it's a very . . . pathetic description." Also, she takes care in pronouncing all the consonants in words, so her words sound "crispier," with shorter and sharper sounds—a word like "and" would sound somewhat like "ant." In general, this is how she would speak in a conversation, but when she is reading a Latin passage or translating a passage, her voice becomes louder, her words very expressive, and there is a wider range of pitch. For example, "graviter commotus" would be spoken with a lower pitch, more slowly, sounding very serious, while something like "Cornelia lacrimat" would be accompanied by a crying voice. Out of all of Mrs. Newman's speech characteristics, these suprasegmentals are probably the thing that catches most Latin students' attention first.

Equally as attention-grabbing as the suprasegmentals is Mrs. Newman's body language. While talking or lecturing, she looks like a normal teacher, leaning against her desk, holding her book in one hand while gesturing with the other. However, when she is reading a story or translating, she acts out the story for the students in the front of the classroom while she speaks. It is not uncommon for her to wave her arms around, stamp her feet, pretend to perform actions of the characters, and point at invisible objects while she tells the story. Of all the characteristics of Mrs. Newman's language, this is definitely the one that she is most famous for—everyone knows what story time with Mrs. Newman is like.

Because of all her different language characteristics—vocabulary, grammar, suprasegmentals, and body language, everyone thinks that Mrs. Newman is a neat teacher. If she did not have these unusual speech habits, it is certain that people would not like her class as much. Who wants to listen to a boring lecture by some college professor when you could have Mrs. Newman act it out for you?

Commentary

The writer presents an excellent introduction, capturing the four main points of the organizational structure, and then proceeds to touch on each point—"First," "another typical aspect," "the third thing," "equally as attention-grabbing." All of this flows easily, without any sense of a checklist of points.

The selection of interesting details breathes life into these points. In fact, the extensive detail on each point suggests careful observation and preplanning in the work of this writer.

In addition, the writer knows the subject of the essay quite well, both the person and the concept of language structure. For example, the writer recognizes that "correct grammar" can make people "appear to be well educated," suggesting that grammar is not necessarily all there is to a good education. Furthermore, the writer introduces "suprasegmentals" and then shows us that he or she knows what "suprasegmentals" are all about.

Finally, each of these four points about language use leads us to a personality trait or some typical association with the person ("Everyone knows what story time with Mrs. Newman is like"), bringing together the language details and the overall portrait of this memorable person. The conclusion adds an emphatic restatement, challenging the readers out there ("you") to make a choice between "a boring lecture by a college professor" and having "Mrs. Newman act it out for you."

Exemplar

Middle

R u b r i c

Cognition: The writer is fluent. In addition, the writer appears to have followed some topic headings or outlines in the development of ideas.

Rhetoric: A clear purpose is not stated at the beginning. The writer seems to drift from one idea to another. Several points are given without any overall framework to guide the reading. Some ideas may be repeated too often.

Linguistics/Conventions: The sentence structure is adequate, but the flow from one sentence to another may be somewhat choppy. The writer has an adequate basic knowledge of conventions. Spelling is a small problem overall.

Themes/Ideas: The paper has some interesting details and suggestions, but these details and suggestions are not conceptualized as ideas.

C o m m e n t a r y

The writer uses excellent details in a four-point organizational pattern (volume, body language, change, expression), but does not give us an introduction outlining the overall organization of the paper. The four points are not always separate categories. Volume (paragraph two) and expressive language (last paragraph) seem to overlap. In addition, the writer does not give us a conclusion bringing these four points together in a memorable image or quotation. The absence of a title is another indication of the failure to present an overall point.

The writer does use excellent details about the father's language use, and these details are excellent evidence

My father is Ethiopian, and he has a very apparent Ethiopian accent. Amharic (his native language) is phonetic so he tends to pronounce each syllable, consonant, and vowel distinctively. For example, my father says "wor-led" instead of our pronunciation of "world", and he says "Connect-i-cut" instead of our pronunciation, emitting the second "c". Also, my father says many words incorrectly. He says "penality" instead of "penalty" and "probablity" instead of "probability".

My father speaks in a moderate volume. He's never too loud or too soft. When he tries to emphasize something, he gets louder and uses many inflections, but it still isn't overbearing. My father's voice changes when he speaks about his children. He gets softer and more serious, and there is a loving expression on his face. My father is very articulate; sounding out each and ever word well.

My father's body language depends upon what mood he i s and which topic he is speaking about. When resting, my father lays with his back against the couch and his arm either resting on his lap or on the armrest. Sometimes he puts both hands behind his head, and he stretches out. When my father is trying to emphasize something, he gets really expressive. He throws his hands about, and he snaps his fingers occasionally. When my father is speaking directly to one person , he tends to put one of his hands on the opposite person's shoulder, and he uses lots of eye contact. There are other small things I notice when observing my father. When he gets mad, he tosses his head about. Also, when my father is listening attentively, he leans forward.

My father's body language really changes when he i s speaking about one of his favorite topics: funny stories about me or the good ole' days. When my father is recanting funny stories about me, his eyes squint with glee, he smiles a lot, and he folds over in laughter. My father is very active when he speaks about the old days. He has a slight grin on his face all the time. He uses his hands a lot and tends to use a lot of physical contact. Also, when he remembers something funny, he bounces in his seat a lot.

My father is very expressive in his language. His background really shows in his speaking and body language. Now when my father finally gets to read this story, he'll probably use his favorite expression: "Lord have mercy!"

for the point under consideration. In this paper, the writer seems to have engaged in extensive observation and analysis before writing the final draft.

Part of the story here is the cultural gap between the Ethiopian father and the American child, a gap which closes when the two bond together as father and child. The "loving expression" in the father's face, "the funny stories about me," with "glee" in his eyes—these detailed moments capture the love underlying this portrait. This is a very good paper, and with more attention to editing and overall organization, this writer could easily write a high paper.

Exemplar — Low

I decided to make a linguistic portrait of my cousin, Samantha. She is almost ten and lives in Chicago, so I had to talk to her by the phone. Samantha seemed to like to talk about her games and school, "things to do" as she put it.

She has a high pitch voice, and talks pretty loud at times and very soft at others, depending on how exited she is about what she's talking about. When she's very happy and likes the topic she gets very energetic with the conversation, with a chipper tone to her voice. But other times, when she doesn't like the topic or would rather be somewhere else, she seems sullen and speaks very softly and seems to avoid eye contact.

Sam has a variety of unusual pronunciations. One such irregularity is in the way she pronounces the word bird, in place of the "i" sound a "u" is put, making it sound like burd. She also say's flower with more a u sound, producing flewer. When saying her, she sounds it with and ar instead of and er, making "har". When answering a question she will reply with a short "yap" to say yes. She will sometimes gloss over the articulation, so the listener may have to have a few words repeated.

R u b r i c

Cognition: Many low papers show no evidence of drafting and planning. Most students use ideas from the class discussion of the topic, but the low writers barely go beyond the point they are making.

Rhetoric: In many low papers, about the time the main idea is beginning to emerge, the writer quits writing. The paper has an informal beginning, but no elaborated introduction to the topic and no overall organizational plan.

Linguistics/Conventions: Run-ons, punctuation, spelling—these are just a few of the conventions which the writer does not use. The overall text structure is often list-like.

Themes/Ideas: The idea of the paper is elusive until nearly the end. The absence of a title could be a clue that the writer is uncertain about the idea at the center of the paper.

Paper continued on page 10

> Samantha has little use for filler words. It seems that she always has something to say and rarely ever pauses during a conversation. If she needs time to think over an answer she will a emit a long ummm . . . and look around the room for a bit until she is ready to speak.
>
> She uses relatively short words. Preferring to say a lot of little words instead of a few big words, which is standard for a nine year old. Over Samantha has a very interesting speech pattern, and is never a dull conversationalist.

Commentary

There are a few structural missteps, but this low writer is showing substantial progress in mastery of conventions (subject-verb agreement, punctuation, quotation marks, pronoun reference and case, spelling, and so forth) and in developing secondary points with concrete evidence. The pronunciation examples are excellent, with two exceptions. One exception is the paragraph on filler words. The writer never gives us a concrete example of the absence of filler words. Another example of lack of evidence is the last paragraph on short words. Some examples would help these assertions. What this low writer does not do is identify from the beginning a controlling idea for the whole essay and elaborate on the organizational plan of the paper. Instead, we get some passing details about age, location, and so forth. This writer begins with a casual "I decided to make a linguistic portrait," but *why* and *how* will the portrait be carried out? No comment. The conclusion makes a weak stab at a generalization, but too late.

The writer of this portrait appears to miss some opportunities to capture the overall impressions of this nine-year-old child. For example, the writer must have had something in mind when he or she says that Samantha "is never a dull conversationalist." Show us! Nevertheless, this is a writer who is making substantial progress and who presents evidence of excellent potential as a writer.

Connections to Standards

	STANDARDS											
	1	2	3	4	5	6	7	8	9	10	11	12
Targeted	1	2	3	//4//	//5//	//6//	7	8	//9//	10	11	12
Supplementary	//1//	//2//	//3//	4	5	6	//7//	//8//	9	10	//11//	//12//

A report-of-information task targets writing standards 4, 5, and 6. This particular task–to produce a linguistic portrait–also targets standard 9. If this task were embedded into a larger unit of classroom instruction, students might also read and respond to various literary and nonliterary texts (1, 2) and apply various strategies as they interpret and evaluate these texts (3). Students might conduct research (7) and use a variety of resources to gather and synthesize information and to create and communicate knowledge (8). Students can use reports of information such as the linguistic portrait to accomplish their own purposes, which might include exploring their own life histories or creating a class publication (11, 12).

Task

To assess a student's capacity to compose an effective argument, teachers in this task asked twelfth graders to argue for or against a proposal by their local school board allowing school administrators to search students' lockers and personal belongings for drugs. According to this proposal, students possessing drugs would be subject to arrest. Twelfth graders were asked to express their views about the proposal in an essay that hypothetically would be sent to the school board. In this particular persuasive task, the students were asked to weigh whether the proposal would affect individual rights and whether it would help control the potential drug problem in schools.

Exemplar — **High**

> Our country has certain qualities which separate it from many others in the world. One of these is our Constitution and its amendments. This piece of work represents our ideal of a nation whose principals are based on free-choice, good of the whole, and individual rights. When individual rights become threatened we often lose our esteem as a great country. This is why I feel that at all times they must be preserved. Our high school is planning to propose a plan where drug searches will be made in lockers and personal belongings of students. Drug sniffing dogs will also help in the search. I'll show in this essay how these action violate every students individual rights, and how the school can't possibly do this legally.
>
> Our Bill of Rights contains the 1st ten amendments to our Constitution. The fourth (2.) prevents the use of illegal search and seizure. By carrying out the proposal the school would be violating this amendment. Every student has his/her own right to privacy, especially at school, a time they get away from home pressures. According to local

Rubric

Cognition: The writing is fluent and the paper suggests that the writer has some excellent planning strategies.

Rhetoric: The text shows outstanding rhetorical awareness. The writer gives the audience room to move to a new position and does not shut off all options.

Linguistics/Conventions: The writer has excellent control of conventions (spelling excellent, grammar fine, punctuation good). The text structure is adequate. The words marking transitions suggest that the writer has a good sense of overall structures.

Themes/Ideas: The development of the ideas provides an interesting argument, but the logic of the ideas may need another revision.

11

Paper continued on page 12

Commentary

The writer, after beginning with a constitutional background for the main point, focuses on the importance of individual rights, especially the amendment preventing illegal search and seizure. But when presenting evidence for not violating this amendment, the writer pleads for the value of tradition and the assertion that "the strength of our whole is in each of us individually." The rhetorical flourishes here are impressive, but the strength of evidence may be in doubt.

But the writer saves what could be a weakened argument at this point by suggesting a new approach for the board. The writer, recognizing the plight of the audience (the board) after the first approach is removed, suggests a student network and a hotline. The writer seems to have substituted student informers for drug-sniffing dogs, suggesting that this approach will help the board in "finding probable cause for a search." The conclusion has some uncertain, confusing assertions in the first and second sentences. But the writer closes with a rousing appeal for a "closer, healthier, popular nation." Good audience sense, strong control of conventions, excellent understanding of many of the ideas—all of these features justify a high ranking. At the end, some questions remain, however, about these student informers. Why are they a more noble choice? These ideas need to be examined again.

law our officials need probable cause to violate the search and seizure clause. By doing these mandatory checks, the board will need no probable cause, and will be granted power to still further the search. As you can see the proposal violates many of our founding beliefs and ideas. Our country has been standing strong for 200 years and I believe there's a reason. I believe we have stayed with the values our forefathers portrayed, over all this time. To violate them now could lead to a dislike of our leaders & officials. We do not need to start restructuring our ideals now. The strength of our whole is in each of us individually.

Next I'd like to propose that the Board restructure its bid. I feel the need for action is neccessary with the drug problem. However we cannot violate individual rights in doing so. I think the board needs to possibly look into a student network, or anonymous hot-line. These two programs could show the school the prime suspects and the board could concentrate their powers on finding probable cause for a search. I believe this way our rights are kept and even a major problem will still be fought.

In Conclusion I hope you see my point with this issue. The drug-search proposal violates our rights guaranteed to us from the day we were born. I do think however our board needs to look for new ways to combat the drug problem. All of these I feel will probate a closer, healthier, popular nation.

My opinion on the subject of searching through lockers and personal belongings, is that this is an invasion of privacy.

Although many people may think that this is a good idea, it shows that no one has trust in teenagers today. This lowers their confidence and self-esteem

As far as the drug-sniffing dogs are concerned, that is not a bad idea. If there were any drugs in the school, they would be found by the dogs, and not by people searching through other people's personal belongings.

I believe that no one trusts kids today. I also believe that this has to stop because even though we are kids, we can tell a wrong from a right. And we know that the desicions we make affect us in every way. Of course, there are some kids that use drugs, drink, and have other bad influences. But it is our desicion to either stay away from them or do what they do.

R u b r i c

Cognition: The development shows some fluency, but it lacks logical consistency, suggesting an absence of overall planning.

Rhetoric: The topic focus needs to be clear in the first paragraph. Audience needs to know in the first paragraph the range of ideas being rejected.

Linguistics/Conventions: There are a few problems of conventions, but overall the writer shows good control of conventions.

Themes/Ideas: The writer develops an idea, proposes an adequate analysis, but evidence is missing.

Commentary

The writer begins with a clear assertion of a personal opinion ("an invasion of privacy") and then provides a strong follow-up ("no one has trust in teenagers"). But the writer begins to weaken those strong beginnings first by trying to explain why absence of trust is bad ("lowers self-esteem") and second by saying that drug-sniffing dogs are "not a bad idea." Why? Because dogs are better searchers.

A similar contradiction develops out of the claim that young people "can tell a wrong from a right" and the claim that some kids "use drugs, drink, and have other bad influences." The writer seems to establish an appropriate distance to audience and to use conventions appropriately most of the time, but loses control of the ideas about halfway through the argument.

Exemplar — Low

Rubric

Cognition: The writer appears not to have an understanding of how to use prewriting processes to generate possible ideas before beginning to write.

Rhetoric: There is no audience awareness.

Linguistics/Conventions: The writer seems to have an adequate sentence sense, but little evidence is presented of any knowledge of larger structures.

Themes/Ideas: The writer seems to ignore most of the ideas in the topic. The one idea presented is not developed.

> I dont think we should have
> drug sniffing dogs because
> I am alergic to dogs.

Commentary

This paper reacts to the idea of drug-sniffing dogs, but does not take a stand on drug searches. This paper gives an initial response and then quits. This writer was asked to consider the dual concepts of the individual and the community. But the writer ignores the larger duality and turns (apparently) to the expressive concern of an allergic reaction.

Connections to Standards

	STANDARDS											
	1	2	3	4	5	6	7	8	9	10	11	12
Targeted	1	2	3	4	5	6	7	8	9	10	11	12
Supplementary	1	2	3	4	5	6	7	8	9	10	11	12

This persuasive task targets writing standards 4, 5, and 6. If a persuasive task were embedded into a larger unit of classroom instruction, students might also read and respond to literary and nonliterary texts (1, 2) and apply various strategies as they interpret and evaluate these texts (3). Students might conduct research (7) and use a variety of resources to gather and synthesize information to create and communicate knowledge about a topic of interest (8). Depending on topics and focus, persuasive tasks can help students develop an understanding of and respect for diversity (9) and to use language to accomplish their own purposes (12), such as influencing school policy or taking a position on a political issue.

RESPONSE TO LITERATURE (ANALYSIS–COMPARISON/CONTRAST)

T a s k

To assess the student's capacity to engage in in-depth reading, including both comprehension and interpretation, the teacher uses a task requiring comparison and contrast of characters. Using details from the play *The Glass Menagerie,* students were asked to arrange the dream worlds of Tom, Laura, and Amanda on a continuum, comparing and contrasting the "reality" of these worlds. Which character is the most insulated from reality? Which least? Which character has the best chance of ultimately reestablishing contact with reality? (Some school sites using this assessment dropped this last question.) This task requires that the reader organize a comparison and contrast of characters, using the continuum as the framework. In this task, students are asked to go beyond appearances and personal experience in order to understand what "degrees of reality" could mean, and to focus carefully on the revealing moments of the play.

Exemplar High

R u b r i c

Cognition: The writer is quite fluent and appears to have good planning strategies.

Rhetoric: The writer understands the necessary tensions of narrative and dramatic structure and has a keen sense of the compelling moment.

Linguistics/Conventions: The student has the basics under control and shows an excellent overall sense of organizational structure.

Themes/Ideas: This writer understands literary themes—how difference tells us about ourselves, how appearance can disguise underlying realities.

Glass Menagerie

There is little doubt as to how I would rate these characters in terms of contact with reality. Tom is the most realistic, followed by Laura, and then Amanda.

Tom is the most realistic. This is evident in his attitudes toward his family, himself, and their relationship with the "outside" world. He has faced the facts: he realizes Laura is crippled, that she is destined to play the victrola for the next 50 years, that is mother is in a lost world, and that he is not moving ahead. He is dissatisfied with his lot—he wishes to do more than stack shoes, smoke and go to the movies. In realizing that his family is in part holding him back, Tom is very much in touch with the real situation.

This being in touch with life, this actual *living* is what distinguishes Tom from Laura. Laura recognized her defects, but resolves to do nothing. She resigns herself to the fact that there will be no gentlemen callers. When questioned by Jim as to what she does, she replies:

"I don't do anything—much. Oh, please dont think I sit around doing nothing! My glass collection takes up a good deal of time. Glass is something you have to take good care of."

In other words, she really *does* do nothing. The fact that she can consider playing with glass a worthy pastime for six years shows she is warped in her sense of judgement. When Jim tries to bring her back to reality, he almost succeeds. But when the truth is known, and he hastily exits, Laura's first reaction is

Paper continued on page 16

15

Commentary

This writer's engagement with the text is evident in the clarity of the opening sentence. He or she then confidently ranks the characters of *The Glass Menagerie,* placing Amanda as the most remote from reality. Through numerous examples presented in the second paragraph, the writer implies a definition of "realistic," which he or she makes explicit in the third paragraph as "being in touch with life . . . actual *living*. . . ."

The strengths of this paper include the directness and clarity of its approach to the assignment; the competent writing skills; the tightness of the total organization; and the careful transitions from paragraph to paragraph. The examples and quotations selected from the text convincingly support this writer's argument.

While this writer makes his or her case in part by ignoring some of the facts of the play (not an uncommon strategy in literary analysis), this paper is not distorted in its treatment of the characters. This writer's insight into literary themes, understanding of the structure of the drama as well as the structure of persuasion, concise style, and control of conventions place this paper in the high range of performance.

to wind the victrola—proof that she is withdrawing once again, and probably forever.

While Laura at least recognizes the fact that she will receive no gentlemen callers, that she is crippled, and that her mother is living in the past, her mother refuses to accept any of these things. Holding on to the blind faith that *her* children cannot be run-of-the-mill, surely not inferior, but *will* make their way in the world, Amanda shows she is totally lost by saying, ". . . Stay fresh and pretty! —Its almost time for our gentlemen callers to start arriving. How many do you think we're going to entertain this afternoon? . . . . . What? No-one—not one? You must be joking. Not one gentleman caller? It can't be true! There must have a flood, there must have been a tornado.

Aside from this belief that something will happen even if they do nothing, Amanda is also superstitious—constantly referring to ways to stay healthy, or wishing on the moon. She is constantly referring to her past in the Blue Mountains—not realizing that this does not apply to a daughter called Blue Roses because of pleurosis—not her beauty.

In short, Tom is the most realistic as he alone realizes his plight, his surroundings, and attempts to leave them. Laura, too, at times realizes her plight, and as with Tom, realizes her mother is lost to reality. She, however, is able to withdraw from reality—something Tom cannot do—and what Amanda does almost constantly.

16

Exemplar — **Middle**

In the play *The Glass Menagerie,* all of the main characters—Tom, Laura, and Amanda—live in a dream world. The character who seems most insulated from reality is Laura. The one whose dream comes closest to reality is Tom's. Laura's world is one closed in by the walls of her home. Her life consists of her glass menagerie, phonograph records, her scrapbook, and her memories of Jim. The glass menagerie is something she can care for, something to have some pride in. Her phonograph records, which were left by her father, give her the enjoyment which she doesn't receive often at home. Because of her crippled condition, she feels there is a barrier between the outside world and the time she spends at home.

The second of the three main characters is Amanda whose "dream world" is retold in the past. From her seventeen gentleman at Blue Mountain to the Governor's Ball, she expresses her experiences all of wonderful times. She retells them as a dream that most girls would live for. One of her experiences might have been the time when she would pick jonquils and would make gentleman callers get out of their carriages to help her. This is the world she now dreams of. It is a world of love and happiness, which is in her life no longer.

The third and final main character is Tom, whose world lies in present and in the future. The most obvious part of his present dream world is the movies. The movies are his escape from life. They are something he can go and leave all his troubles outside. He gives many reasons for attending the movies so frequently, and his stock explanation is that he likes "adventure". He says he like adventure because it is one thing he sees little of at home or at work. Another one of his escapes is his smoking. He feels that by smoking he can get away from all of the world. For him it is a time to relax his tensions and put himself at ease. His dream of the future is to be a writer. He writes poems in some of his spare time, this is the only hobby he has. It is the only way of expressing himself. Thus the dream worlds of these characters differ and each does something for him.

Rubric

Cognition: The writer is fluent.
Rhetoric: The writer offers a set of information to explain a response, but lacks some awareness of the telling moment, the telling comment or gesture, which captures the spirit of a literary experience.
Linguistics/Conventions: Good grasp of basics in both reading and composition.
Themes/Ideas: The writer understands important literary themes—the idea of insulation from reality, the differences between appearance and reality.

Commentary

This writer establishes a context for the paper by naming the three main characters and claiming that all live in a "dream world." The writer then ranks them from "most insulated" from reality to "closer to reality." The examples of Laura's dream world are accurate, but the writer does not fully explain how these examples make Laura the character most insulated from reality.

The transition to Amanda is clear but not skillful. Here again, the writer does not fully explain the link between the examples given from the text and how Amanda's "dream world" is somehow less insulated than Laura's. The discussion of Tom follows a similar pattern. This writer hints at some insight into the links between reality and characters who live in the past, present, future, or simply a fantasy world.

This paper has very few errors of language structure and conventions. The writing is competent but not distinctive in either diction or sentence structure. This middle-level paper is thoughtful and sincere, even if predictable in language and content.

Exemplar

Low

R u b r i c

Cognition: The writer appears to do little drafting or prewriting before beginning the final copy.

Rhetoric: The writer addresses the audience but seems to include too many facts that leave the audience wondering what the point of the essay is. The voice throughout the essay is inconsistent. Missing throughout is an adequate sense of overall organization.

Linguistics/Conventions: The writer produces a range of errors, both in structures and in conventions. Nevertheless, the writer does have some sense of sentence structure.

Themes/Ideas: The opening sentence has a promising focus, but the focus begins to slip away as ideas become vague. Nevertheless, the student shows some insight here and there, suggesting that this writer is making progress but needs more practice and helpful guidance.

The most insulated from reality is Laura. She plays with her glass menagerie, and plays her old records over and over again. As soon as Laura walks into her room, she is in her own little world, shut off from reality. In scene one you start to find a little bit about Laura. Act two scene I Jim is introduced into the story and into Laura's life. The name Blue Roses is part of her dream world. Jim called her blue Roses because Laura was sick with pleurosis and when she got back he thought she said Blue Roses. Laura always kept a little scrap Book, it was so neat, and everything had its own little place, just like her dream world.

Amanda dream world was not as insulated as Lauras. By the means of escape she would always talk about her past, Her Gentlemen callers "seventeen" of them so she says. It was up at Blue Mountain she'd always talk about it. She'd want to make a picnic and get away with her family.

Amanda was always busy making some kinds of plans for Laura, either wanting her to date or having to sit and stay neat & pretty for her gentlemen callers. And how excited she got when she heard Tom was bringing home a boy for Laura. She fixed new lamp shades, and went over the furnature a little, she made alot of declious food, and that dress she wore, that dress she had worn on the day She met Laura's father. She was trying to hard to make a good impression. In scene I act two is where Amanda fixes the lamps and furinature. That scene is where she wore that dress.

Toms dream world is filled with adventure thats why he goes to the movies so often, and he also goes by means of escape. Tom's wanting to become a writter in the first few scenes you notice that. He enjoys doing something else besides going to the movies. going out onto the fire escape was another mean of escape for tom. Tom would use the fire escape like the new world, not the world of adventure he see's in the movies. Both Laura and Tom use the fire escape.

It something that they know is always there. Tom snokes alot, sometimes he's nervous and other times he smokes for another escape, throughout the whole play Tom is smoking and using the fire escape, and going to the movies.

In the play the character Tom, I think has the best of ultimately reestablishing contact with reality. Tom can face alot of things more than Amanda or Laura can like; facing the fact that by bringing Jim over it wouldn't help or change matters at all, in fact he was aganist it or unconserned about the whole idea from the beginning, because he knew it wouldn't help. He wants to get out on his own you know then that he's trying to feel for something but he's still not sure of what he wants, but he knows he wants to get out into the world. In my opinion I think he will make it.

Commentary

This writer does not establish a context for writing and does not present a focusing statement for the paper. The writer demonstrates some understanding of the play beyond a literal level and at times shows insights which transcend the overall poor performance in this paper (e.g., explaining the symbolism of Laura's scrapbook, noting the fact that both Laura and Tom use the fire escape). This writer sometimes cites examples from the play which do little to advance his or her argument; the discussion of Amanda is especially jumbled and at times redundant.

There is a range of errors in both structures and conventions; nevertheless, the writing is quite fluent and the paper longer than most low-range performances. With help in organization and editing, this student could probably move to a higher level of performance.

NOTE: Some teachers liked this assignment, but many teachers objected to it on the following grounds: (1) the wording is needlessly "formidable"; (2) the directions fail to indicate what kind of "continuum" is meant; (3) the student can only guess about which character has the best chance of reestablishing contact with reality; but (4) if you leave out that part of the assignment, the student is being asked to do little more than to summarize what he or she has already probably discussed in class. The task could be structured so that students have no discussion before writing on the topic. Revised assignments were prepared to meet these objections.

The samples written in response to the original assignment indicate the students' disagreement about which character is most remote from reality. The usual arrangement is Tom, Amanda, and Laura—in increasing order of remoteness—yet some *high* papers made a persuasive case for Amanda as the most remote, and one teacher reported that some of his students thought Tom was the most remote because he was still living in a dream world years after the play's ending. Putting aside their personal convictions, the judges tried to rate each paper in terms of how persuasively it presents whatever viewpoint it chooses to present. Teachers reported that the original assignment, although difficult, did produce some very interesting papers. One of the popular revised assignments, incidentally, was the following:

> The epigraph to the play is the last line of e.e. cummings's "somewhere i have never traveled," which is "nobody, not even the rain, has such small hands." What may be some of the reasons that Williams selected that line as his epigraph? How do the words relate to the play?

Connections to Standards

	STANDARDS											
Targeted	1	2	3	4	5	6	7	8	9	10	11	12
Supplementary	1	2	3	4	5	6	7	8	9	10	11	12

This comparison/contrast task targets students' skills at reading literature in depth (2) and writing a formal analysis in response to their reading (4, 5). This task requires students to apply their knowledge of language structure, language conventions, figurative language, and genre (6). As students acquire and develop skill in reading and interpreting literature, they might use a variety of reading strategies (3). Students might also conduct research on literary topics of interest (e.g., reading literary criticism) and/or viewing film or live performance of a work (7, 8). This particular task could be extended by having students perform or direct scenes from the drama based on their interpretations of the main character, or to share their interpretations in literary discussion groups (11, 12).

RESPONSE TO LITERATURE (ANALYSIS)

Task

The assessment of response to literature usually emphasizes (1) range of reading, (2) in-depth reading of one selection, (3) intertextual reading, or (4) the literary traditions informing U.S. culture. This task for assessing response to literature asked students to describe how one of the main characters changes in a selected novel or play. The emphasis was on in-depth reading of one selection. Notice that both this task and the previous one are assessing analysis. The previous one analyzed contrasts and comparisons among three characters. This task analyzes one character over time.

Exemplar — High

Rubric

Cognition: The writer is fluent and seems to have a good command of various organizing strategies.

Rhetoric: The writer clearly spells out the thesis of the essay at the beginning, giving the reader a clear guide for what follows.

Linguistics/Conventions: The writer has an excellent understanding of language structure at the level of word choice, sentence structures, and overall text structure. Excellent control of conventions.

Themes/Ideas: The writer understands central literary concepts like irony, self-knowledge, hearsay, civilization. In addition, the writer is able to bring together generalities and concrete evidence around the concept of change over time.

Kurtz, in Joseph Conrad's *The Heart of Darkness* is an example of a character who goes through a trying ordeal and gains a deeper knowledge of himself. The story itself is narrated by a seaman name Marlow, through whose eyes the reader sees Kurtz. Kurtz is introduced by hearsay as a universal genius. He is a bright young man sent into the heart of African darkness to gain experience in the trade of ivory and write a social report on native customs. His purpose is to gain self-education and self-knowledge.

The full irony of this situation is recognized when Marlow first meets Kurtz face to face. A row of dried heads on stakes around Kurtze's jungle hut testifies to the knowledge he has gained. Instead of leading the natives toward the civilization of the Europeans Kurtz has lost all trace of his old ways and become a king among the savages—a bloody tyrant of the darkness.

This condition does not seem to show any self knowledge, and certainly while Kurtz is among the natives he does not worry about knowing himself. And yet when, as a dying man, he is enclosed in the cabin of a small river boat slowly winding its way back toward civilization. Mr. Kurtz is forced to consider. In the jungle he had considered only the values and those of the world he left were allowed to slip away and become deformed. When his former way of life—the way of Europe—forces itself upon him he is forced to re-examine his actions and his double set of values. Conrad states that even the most civilized of men has a savage side of his personality he generally keeps subdued. Kurtz, on the other hand, has let his evil side dominate and has stepped one pace over the brink that separates civilized man from the animals. The trying experience of dying a slow death among his own people but as an outcast causes Kurtz to re-examine himself. He goes from a state of defending his own actions and demanding "only justice" for himself to a state of abject recognition. His final words are "The horror! The horror!" Kurtz truly gains self-knowledge by a trying experience and re-examination of his own values. But this is an ironic, tragic knowledge that comes for him much too late.

Commentary

This paper suggests that its writer has a perceptive understanding of a challenging work and a keen awareness of the demands of the task. The organization of the paper responds directly to the task, using relevant and illuminating details. The wording is exact, the sentence structure is solid, and the style is controlled.

The writer defines the ironic contrast between the character's actual experiences in the African jungle and his original pretension in coming there. With similar insight, the student defines the ordeal of the boat ride back to the civilization that Kurtz allegedly betrayed and Kurtz's ultimate realization not only of that alleged betrayal but also of what it does to him.

The detail used is outstanding for its sharpness and its appropriateness. The reference to the "row of dried heads on stakes" around Kurtz's hut tellingly underscores the contrast between what the character actually was in the jungle and what the intention was that sent him there. The citing of Kurtz's own final words, "The horror! The horror!" condenses the whole story of agonized self-realization.

The writer works perceptively and accurately through many of the ironies and complexities of the book and of the character. For example, the writer distinguishes between the kind of knowledge of himself, amounting to delusion, that Kurtz has persuaded himself of and the real self-knowledge that finds its anguished expression in "The horror!"

This student, although writing an excellent analysis of Conrad's work, does not focus on some important multicultural concepts about pluralism. The assumptions about Europe and Africa are present without question, for example. Nevertheless this is an excellent, in-depth response to a quality literary selection.

R u b r i c

Cognition: The writer may need practice with strategies for drafting and prewriting.

Rhetoric: The writer does not provide a clear, elaborated thesis at the beginning of the essay.

Linguistics/Conventions: The writer has excellent sentence sense, but the overall organization of the text is weak. The writer has good command of conventions.

Themes/Ideas: The student understands the basic plot of the work but is not able to offer much interpretation of the larger patterns. The student has a general idea about the concept of change over time, but no consistent understanding.

Commentary

This paper meets the demands of the task but lacks the subtlety and insight of the "high" paper. The writer uses appropriate adjectives to comment on characters, but spends too much time summarizing plot unnecessarily. The writer reduces the complexities of Lear's experiences to learning "the true meaning of love." Nevertheless, this student's interpretation recognizes the nature of Lear's blindness, the means by which he is enlightened, and the knowledge he gains.

Whereas the "high" paper focuses on analysis, using elements of the plot only to further that analysis, this paper presents the analysis as a by-product of a chronological and narrative form of organization. The choice of a chronological form of organization may have lessened the writer's chances for presenting a persuasive interpretation of Lear's character.

In the great tragedy, *King Lear,* King Lear is the main character who undergoes important changes in his personality.

As the play opens, King Lear is depicted as a strong-willed, self-centered, impatient man. He has decided to divide his kingdom among his three daughters Goneril, Regan, and Cordelia. Regan and Goneril resort to flattery of Lear in order to get large portions of the kingdom. Lear demonstrates his conceit as he blandly agrees with their ridiculous flattery and he rewards the conniving sisters generously.

Cordelia, on the other hand, speaks the truth to King Lear when she tells him that she cannot flatter him as the other sisters did but she loves him only as a daughter can love her father. Blindly, Lear banishes her for this.

Lear soon begins to realize his mistake when Goneril and Regan refuse to treat him as a king. He is angry and impatient at this filial ingratitude but there is no way for him to remedy the situation. Matters soon get worse when Goneril and Regan finally oust him out of his home onto the heath.

Lear endures much mental torture but with the torture comes self-knowledge and he realizes his mistakes. The plight of Lear is contrasted with the lesser plight of Glouchester, victim of similar ingratitude, who undergoes horrible physical torture which is not as harrowing as Lear's mental torture.

As the tragedy nears its end the reader discovers that King Lear has lost his conceitedness and his overpowering self-will. He has gained some self-knowledge and is now an humble old man who realizes his mistakes.

In the last scenes of the play Lear is reunited with his daughter, Cordelia. Lear has finally learned the true meaning of love but is too late and the play ends with the tragic deaths of Cordelia and King Lear.

Exemplar

Mark Twain's novel *Huckleberry Finn* is a novel in which Twain shows his feelings and values to the reader. In this book Huck shows us the ideas of Twain. About one quarter of the way through the book, the reader sees Huck on a raft with a run away slave, but he would feel worse if he were to betray such a good friend a Jim (who is the slave.) This is possibly showing that not only does Twain possess a great deal of loyalty to his friends, but he has also educated himself to a point where he can make up his own mind without the influence of social prejudices. Twain also shows us a recognition of his strength in handling people. The ability to figure out what kind of a person someone is goes hand in hand with this. This is shown in the book when Huck and Jim pick up the two men who posed as royalty Huck immediately figures them out, but does not let them or Jim know this. In an earlier part of the book, Twain expresses his dislike for social "straight-jackets." This is shown when he pictures Huck enjoying life with his father rather than with his aunt. Twain said Huck could smoke and swear whenever he wished with his father, but not so with his aunt. Also at the end of the book Huck after running away must return to society and rules which will bind him. There are several other illustrations such as this but time and space do not allow for them.

Rubric

Cognition: This low writer is more fluent than most and appears to have some preplanning strategies. Typically, low writers are fragmented in their processing of information.

Rhetoric: The student does not have a clear sense of the overall structure of the literary work, and does not present a clear organizational structure.

Linguistics/Conventions: The writer has some sense of sentence structure, but loses control here and there. Confusing pronoun references, punctuation problems, and other editing problems undermine the quality of the paper.

Themes/Ideas: The student does not address the assigned topic and does not have a clear understanding of the central concepts of the novel. The writer touches on some important ideas, but goes on, not stopping to think deeply about any point.

Commentary

This paper suggests that the writer has some knowledge of *Huckleberry Finn* and can formulate interpretations of key events in the novel. However, this writer has not responded directly to the task. The writer confuses author with character throughout the paper and provides a seemingly random list of details from the novel, which do not add up to a convincing and coherent interpretation of character.

Connections to Standards

	STANDARDS											
Targeted	1	2	3	4	5	6	7	8	9	10	11	12
Supplementary	1	2	3	4	5	6	7	8	9	10	11	12

This response-to-literature task targets students' skills at reading literature in depth (2) and writing a formal analysis in response to their reading (4, 5). This task requires students to apply their knowledge of language structure, language conventions, figurative language, and genre (6). As students acquire and develop skill in reading and interpreting literature, they might use a variety of reading strategies (3). Students might also conduct research on literary topics of interest (e.g., reading literary criticism); they might view and respond to film or live performance of a work (7, 8). Films based on these three works are available. This particular task could be extended by having students choose an alternative method of communicating their interpretations (e.g., poems, paintings, dramatization) and sharing these with their peers (11, 12).

RESPONSE TO LITERATURE (INTERTEXTUALITY)

T a s k

In the two previous tasks, students were asked to compare and contrast characters and then contrast changes in one character over time. Another important skill in response to literature is the capacity to comprehend and interpret common patterns which occur in different kinds of texts—paintings, poems, myths, and so forth. In this task, students were asked to write a comparison and contrast of the Icarus myth, the Brueghel painting *The Fall of Icarus,* and W. H. Auden's poem "Musée des Beaux Arts." Students were asked to explain specifically in what way the three treatments are similar and different in content or facts, in purpose, and in tone. The topic is, among other things, attempting to help students understand the intertextuality of art—the way works of art influence and interact with each another. A description of a teaching unit on the myth, the poem, and the Brueghel painting can be found in the March 1989 issue of *English Journal,* an NCTE publication. A copy of the Brueghel painting is in the same article.

Exemplar High

R u b r i c

Cognition: The student is obviously a fluent reader and writer. The smoothness of the paper suggests the writer used some planning and drafting strategies in both the reading and writing.

Rhetoric: From the beginning the writer presents a clear focus for the reader but without telling the whole story.

Linguistics/Conventions: The top writer has good control of conventions and language structure. There may be awkward phrasing here and there, but there are no consistent missteps in conventions and structure.

Themes/Ideas: The writer presents a complex analysis of the intertextuality of the texts, combining both similarities and differences. Throughout the essay, the top writer moves easily between the generalities of ideas and concrete details.

The Fall of Icarus: Myth, Painting, and Poem

Reading Auden's poem about Brueghel's painting about the mythological fall of Icarus and realizing this history is like coming upon a flower from a seed which has been buffeted by the wind for centuries, and which had finally blossomed —not only once but twice!

The ancient Greek tale about Icarus, the brilliant inventor's son, claims that when the father and son were fleeing from the Cretan labyrinth with wings made from feathers and wax, the boy, ignoring his parent's warning, flew too near the sun. The sun melted the wax, and Icarus fell into the sea and drowned.

Although the sixteenth-century painter and the modern poet utilized this drowning, their emphases were slightly different from each other and quite different from the legend. The legend seem to be scolding boys for foolishly disobeying their wise fathers; Brueghel and Auden had another purpose in mind. Brueghel showed a completely indifferent landscape: a farmer is thoughtfully plowing; a shepherd is absently gazing at the sky; sheep are nibbling the grass; ships are sailing in the cove; farmer, shepherd, sheep, and ships are unaware of each other and *a boy falling from the sky. Auden picked up the indifference, almost ignored the painter's ironic humor, and added suffering.*

Brueghel's picture is rather humorous for several reasons. He painted a prominent literary figure as a pair of kicking legs. No one noticed a boy falling out of the sky, which was *"something amazing," as Auden said. The fall seems serious and terrible in the poem. Auden called the situation a "disaster;" he heard a "forsaken cry" and saw "green Water." The water in the painting is a quite gay blue; green sound sickening and cold. In the line, "Something amazing, a boy falling out of the sky," the poet shows the only lightness in the poem. He used the painting to illustrate his idea that suffering occurs while "someone else is eating or opening a window or just walking dully along" and that no one notices the unfortunate one.*

While reading the legend, I did not think about the splash-down; the poem and the painting, however, depend on it. In the myth, Icarus had a personality since he disobeyed his father; in the other two works, he was a distressed pair of legs. Brueghel's Icarus landed in a sixteenth-century landscape: I doubt that any ancient farmer wore a red shirt under a gathered coat.

All these differences in the general plot make the artists' intent clear. One can discover what the man liked and what he rejected in the previous work.

Commentary

The strengths of this extremely competent response to the task are compressed style and keen insight. An example of these qualities is the reference to Brueghel's and Auden's Icarus as a "distressed pair of legs." The summary of Brueghel's painting and Auden's poem in paragraph three is a sample of the paper's richly packed brevity. The metaphor in the opening paragraph is imaginative (although some might argue over its appropriateness). One of the nicest touches in this paper is the recognition in paragraph three that Brueghel's picture is tinged with "ironic humor" and the effectively detailed development of that recognition in paragraph four. The comparison of the water's color in the painting and in the poem is another unexpected and discerning touch. While this student may not have exhausted the possibilities of the task, this paper is outstanding for its clear insight, skillful interpretation, and fluent expression.

Exemplar

Rubric

Cognition: The writer is fluent and sometimes strategic, at least as suggested by some of the transitions.

Rhetoric: The introduction presents a clear thesis to guide the reader, but the writer often confuses the focus of the essay with digressions at the midpoint and at the end.

Linguistics/Conventions: There are some problems with conventions and language structure. Overall text organization is weak.

Themes/Ideas: The writer has a clear grasp of the basic ideas in the individual texts but does not give much attention to the overall complexities of difference and similarity.

Commentary

This "middle" range paper represents an adequate response to the task. The organization is simple with a formulaic introduction, two paragraphs of development, and a conclusion which attempts to leave a question in the mind of the reader. In contrast to the writer of the high paper, this writer states in the opening paragraph that the same general purpose ("expressing their feelings") animates the creators of the myth, the painting, and the poem. Although the paper demonstrates that the writer has some understanding of the three works of art, the interpretation advanced is not fully developed or focused.

"Musée des Beaux Arts"

Auden's poem, Brueghel's painting, and the myth of Icarus are basically telling the same story. Each is concerned with portraying the suffering of man and the indifference of others toward those suffering. The artist, the story teller, and the writer, in their own way, are expressing their feelings.

Inspired by the Greek myth about Icarus and his father Daedalus, Brueghel set out to express his opinion through art. His painting, The Fall of Icarus, *contains much more than the mere plight of Icarus. The indifference of the plowman and the sheppard are clearly evident. Their backs are turned away from human suffering. Perhaps they didn't see his fall, but the man leaning over the water throwing pebbles into the sea and those on board the ship can almost reach out and touch him.*

Almost following a pattern; first the myth, then a visual interpretation, and lastly the written word, Auden expresses himself in his Poem "Musée des Beaux Arts". From the title of the poem and even from the first sentence we can see that Auden is interpreting a work of art. "Old Masters" who understand the human position and suffering include Auden, Brueghel, and even the ancient Greek myth tellers. Lines 14–21 of Auden's poem are directly concerned with Brueghel's painting. He is merely explicating the great work of art.

No matter how the "Old Masters" show us their understanding of human suffering and the indifference of others their messages will always be clear. Whats so amazing about "a boy falling out of the sky?"

Exemplar — Low

> "The Fall of Icarus" in the myth, Brueghel's painting and Auden's poem are all very similar because they treat the fall as lightly as possible. The purpose in the three treatments seems to be very much the same also, because the purpose is to show Icarus he must suffer alone no matter how many times he was told and disobeyed, he only received that one chance. This purpose can very easily be applied to our own lives today that we must suffer alone no matter who we tell our problems to and Brueghel's purpose in his portrait may have been depicting this very purpose for the people after Icarus to follow. The myth, as myths often do, depict some moral and point it out and play it up so as to reach the emotions of its readers. In Auden's poem, Auden treats the fall very lightly and sometimes as I think in this poem, (it) the point Auden is trying to make is emphasized more by treating it as light as possible. The tone in the three treatments is similar because it is serious and has an overall tragic (feeling) tone. The tone is serious and somber and in the painting there is a suffering which is depicted in the fall. Particularly, in the painting, this suffering tone makes you interested as a viewer, and stirs some emotion within each individual. The calm and serene atmosphere in the poem and in the painting creates a lonliness which is difficult to explain, but is certainly there. In contrasting Brueghel's painting, Auden's poem and the myth, I find only similarities which are all in themselves very important and shed much light on the meaning, the purpose and the emotional feeling which the painter, the poet and the myth wanted identified.

Rubric

Cognition: The writing is fluent, but the writer never seems to ask himself or herself "What do I mean by this statement? What is my evidence?"

Rhetoric: The writer does not give a clear focus in the introduction.

Linguistics/Conventions: Pronoun reference problems contribute to the vagueness of the explanations. The sentence sense is questionable (no paragraphing). In general, however, low-range papers often show an adequate control of the basics of most conventions.

Themes/Ideas: Papers at this low level suffer from inconsistency in the central idea or ideas and fail to present concrete details to support generalities.

Commentary

This "low" range response to the task suggests that the writer is confused about purpose, tone, and theme in the three works of art. The writer begins by claiming that the myth, painting, and poem all "treat the fall as lightly as possible," but switches positions about halfway through the paper and claims the three treatments share an "overall tragic (feeling) tone." The paper includes no concrete details or examples to support a vague and contradictory interpretation, leaving the reader to wonder about the extent to which the student has read and understood the texts and the task.

Connections to Standards

	STANDARDS											
Targeted	1	2	3	4	5	6	7	8	9	10	11	12
Supplementary	1	2	3	4	5	6	7	8	9	10	11	12

This response-to-literature task targets students' skills at reading literature in depth (2) and writing a formal analysis in response to their reading (4, 5). This task requires students to apply their knowledge of language structure, language conventions, figurative language, and genre in order to interpret both print and nonprint texts (6). The painting also challenges the students' knowledge of viewing (3, 12). As students acquire and develop skill in reading and interpreting literature, they might use a variety of reading strategies (3). Students might also conduct research on topics of interest (e.g., other literary works that have inspired artistic expression of various kinds, including music and dance) (7, 8). This particular task could be extended by having students choose yet another mode of responding to the Icarus myth (e.g., poems, paintings, dramatization) and sharing these representations with their peers (11, 12).

RESPONSE TO LITERATURE

T a s k

To assess reading processes in response to literature, teachers look for evidence in marginal comments, in first impressions about thoughts and feelings, in comments on figurative language, and in comments on images and symbols. Many of the questions ask students to make personal connections to the text. The following task was taken from "A Sampler of English-Language Arts Assessment–High School" from the California Department of Education.

You are going to read an excerpt from *Black Boy,* an autobiographical work by African American author Richard Wright. This excerpt takes place in the 1920s, when Wright was 18 years old. He was living in a southern city at a time when Blacks were not allowed to use the public library. In the newspaper he read about a controversial author, H. L. Mencken, and wanted to find out more about him. After considering the various white men he knew from where he worked, Wright approached a man he thought was trustworthy. The man lent Wright a library card, and Wright forged notes requesting books from the library. You will be asked to respond to seven prompts about the story.

As you read, you may mark up the selection in any way that helps you better understand or remember what you are reading.

My thoughts, feelings, and/or questions about what I'm reading.*	Excerpt from **Black Boy** by Richard Wright	My thoughts, feelings, and/or questions about what I'm reading.*
*In the test for 1994, this wording has been changed to: My thoughts and/or questions about what I'm reading.		*In the test for 1994, this wording has been changed to: My thoughts and/or questions about what I'm reading.

Student A

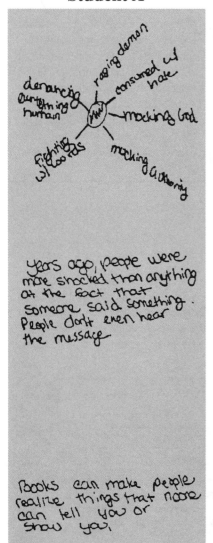

years ago, people were more shocked than anything at the fact that someone said something. People don't even hear the message

Books can make people realize things that noone can tell you or show you.

That night in my rented room, while letting the hot water run over my can of pork and beans in the sink, I opened *A Book of Prefaces* and began to read. I was jarred and shocked by the style, the clear, clean sweeping sentences. Why did he write like that? And how did one write like that? I pictured the man as a raging demon, slashing with his pen, consumed with hate, denouncing everything American, extolling everything European or German, laughing at the weaknesses of people, mocking God, authority. What was this? I stood up trying to realize what reality lay behind the meaning of the words . . . Yes, this man was fighting, fighting with words. He was using words as a weapon, using them as one would use a club. Could words be weapons? Well, yes, for here they were. Then, maybe, perhaps, I could use them as a weapon? No. It frightened me. I read on and what amazed me was not what he said, but how on earth anybody had the courage to say it.

Occasionally I glanced up to reassure myself that I was alone in the room. Who were these men about whom Mencken was talking so passionately? Who was Anatole France? Joseph Conrad? Sinclair Lewis, Sherwood Anderson, Dostoevski, George Moore, Gustave Flaubert, Maupassant, Tolstoy, Frank Harris, Mark Twain, Thomas Hardy, Arnold Bennett, Stephen Crane, Zola, Norris, Gorky, Bergson, Ibsen, Balzac, Bernard Shaw, Dumas, Poe, Thomas Mann, O. Henry, Dreiser, H. G. Wells, Gogol, T. S. Eliot, Gide, Baudelaire, Edgar Lee Masters, Stendhal, Turgenev, Huneker, Nietzsche, and scores of others? Were these men real? Did they exist or had they existed? And how did one pronounce their names?

I ran across many words whose meaning I did not know, and I either looked them up in a dictionary or, before I had a chance to do that, encountered the word in a context that made its meaning clear. But what strange world was this? I concluded the book with the conviction that I had somehow overlooked something terribly important in life. I had once tried to write, had reveled in feeling, had let my crude imagination roam, but the impulse to dream had been slowly beaten out of me by experience. Now it surged up again and I hungered for books, new ways of looking and seeing. It was

Student B

I think he is reading a book written by a very mean person. He is very prejudce and is making fun of every thing but himself.

I think that the author of the book is a very good writer. He writes down exactly what he thinks. He puts his imagination into his books.

28

Student A

Student B

not a matter of believing or disbelieving what I read, but of feeling something new, of being affected by something that made the look of the world different.

As dawn broke I ate my pork and beans, feeling dopey, sleepy. I went to work, but the mood of the book would not die; it lingered, coloring everything I saw, heard, did. I now felt that I knew what the white men were feeling. Merely because I had read a book that had spoken of how they lived and thought, I identified myself with that book.

I felt vaguely guilty. Would I, filled with bookish notions, act in a manner that would make the whites dislike me?

I forged more notes and my trips to the library became frequent. Reading grew into a passion. My first serious novel was Sinclair Lewis's *Main Street*. It made me see my boss, Mr. Gerald, and identify him as an American type. I would smile when I saw him lugging his gold bags into the office. I had always felt a vast distance separating me from the boss, and now I felt closer to him, though still distant. I felt now that I knew him, that I could feel the very limits of his narrow life. And this had happened because I had read a novel about a mythical man called George F. Babbitt.

The plots and stories in the novels did not interest me so much as the point of view revealed. I gave myself over to each novel without reserve, without trying to criticize it; it was enough for me to see and feel something different. And for me, everything was something different. Reading was like a drug, a dope. The novels created moods in which I lived for days. But I could not conquer my sense of guilt, my feeling that the white men around me knew that I was changing, that I had begun to regard them differently.

Whenever I brought a book to the job, I wrapped it in newspaper—a habit that was to persist for years in other cities and under other circumstances. But some of the white men pried into my packages when I was absent and they questioned me.

"Boy, what are you reading those books for?"

"Oh, I don't know, sir."

"That's deep stuff you're reading, boy."

"I'm just killing time, sir."

"You'll addle your brains if you don't watch out."

I read Dreiser's *Jennie Gerhardt* and *Sister Carrie* and they revived in me a vivid sense of my mother's suffering; I was overwhelmed. I grew silent, wondering about the life around me. It would have been impossible for me to have told anyone what I derived from these novels, for it was nothing less than a sense of life itself. All my life had shaped me for the realism, the naturalism of the modern novel, and I could not read enough of them.

Steeped in new moods and ideas, I bought a ream of paper and tried to write; but nothing would come, or what did come was flat beyond telling. I discovered that more than desire and feeling were necessary to write and I dropped the idea. Yet I still wondered how it was possible to know people sufficiently to write about them? Could I ever learn about life and people? To me, with my vast ignorance, my Jim Crow station in life, it seemed a task impossible of achievement. I now knew

Student A annotations:

- I think this boy's boss is a white man and has never even tried to relate to this black kid that works for him.

- People that were other than black brainwashed this kid in thinking that books would "addle his brains".

- I wish I had the desire to read as many books as this person does.

Student B annotations:

He is starting to feel closer to his boss and started to regard some of the other white men differently. He didn't want the white men to know he was reading. They found out and told him to stop.

He was beginning to become adicted to reading novels. He tried to write a book but he didn't have any ideas. He now knows the world is full of hostility and killing.

My thoughts, feelings, and/or
questions about what I'm reading.

Student A

My thoughts, feelings, and/or
questions about what I'm reading.

Student B

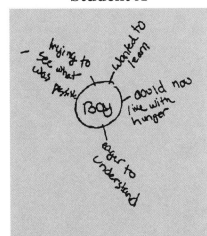

what being a Negro meant. I could endure the hunger. I had learned to live with hate. But to feel that there were feelings denied me, that the very breath of life itself was beyond my reach, that more than anything else hurt, wounded me. I had a new hunger.

In buoying me up, reading also cast me down, made me see what was possible, what I had missed. My tension returned, new, terrible, bitter, surging almost too great to be contained. I no longer *felt* that the world about me was hostile, killing; I *knew* it. A million times I asked myself what I could do to save myself, and there were no answers. I seemed forever condemned, ringed by walls.

I did not discuss my reading with Mr. Falk, who had lent me his library card; it would have meant talking about myself and that would have been too painful. I smiled each day, fighting desperately to maintain my old behavior, to keep my disposition seemingly sunny. But some of the white men discerned that I had begun to brood.

"Wake up there, boy!" Mr. Olin said one day.

"Sir!" I answered for the lack of a better word.

"You act like you've stolen something," he said.

I laughed in the way I knew he expected me to laugh, but I resolved to be more conscious of myself, to watch my every act, to guard and hide the new knowledge that was dawning within me.

If I went north, would it be possible for me to build a new life then? But how could a man build a life upon vague, unformed yearning? I wanted to write and I did not even know the English language. I bought English grammars and found them dull. I felt that I was getting a better sense of the language from novels than from grammars. I read hard, discarding a writer as soon as I felt that I had grasped his point of view. At night the printed page stood before my eyes in sleep.

Mrs. Moss, my landlady, asked me one Sunday morning:

"Son, what is this you keep on reading?"

"Oh, nothing. Just novels."

"What you get out of 'em?"

"I'm just killing time," I said.

"I hope you know your own mind," she said in a tone which implied that she doubted if I had a mind.

I knew of no Negroes who read the books I liked and I wondered if any Negroes ever thought of them. I knew that there were Negro doctors, lawyers, newspapermen, but I never saw any of them. When I read a Negro newspaper I never caught the faintest echo of my preoccupation in its pages. I felt trapped and occasionally, for a few days, I would stop reading. But a vague hunger would come over me for books, books that opened up new avenues of feeling and seeing, and again I would forge another note to the white librarian. Again I would read and wonder as only the naive and unlettered can read and wonder, feeling that I carried a secret, criminal burden about with me each day.

That winter my mother and brother came and we set up housekeeping, buying furniture on the installment

— Reading shooldn't be a crime and why dose this boy have to tell people he's just killing time? Reading is more Than that to him.

He doesn't know of any other negroes that like the kinds of book he likes. They began saving money so they can make a trip north. He thinks he can start a new life there and write books

Student A

This person's life was sculpted by the white people around him and it woud offend them to know that he wasn't happy with it.

"If I did not want others to violate my life, how could I voluntarily vidate it myself?"

"I wondered how long I could bear the tension, anxiety & terror."

plan, being cheated and yet knowing no way to avoid it. I began to eat warm food and to my surprise found that regular meals enabled me to read faster. I may have lived through many illnesses and survived them, never suspecting that I was ill. My brother obtained a job and we began to save toward the trip north, plotting our time, setting tentative dates for departure. I told none of the white men on the job that I was planning to go north; I knew that the moment they felt I was thinking of the North they would change toward me. It would have made them feel that I did not like the life I was living, and because my life was completely conditioned by what they said or did, it would have been tantamount to challenging them.

I could calculate my chances for life in the South as a Negro fairly clearly now.

I could fight the southern whites by organizing with other Negroes, as my grandfather had done. But I knew that I could never win that way; there were many whites and there were but few blacks. They were strong and we were weak. Outright black rebellion could never win. If I fought openly I would die and I did not want to die. News of lynchings were frequent.

I could submit and live the life of a genial slave, but that was impossible. All of my life had shaped me to live by my own feelings and thought. I could make up to Bess and marry her and inherit the house. But that, too, would be the life of a slave; if I did that, I would crush to death something within me, and I would hate myself as much as I knew the whites already hated those who had submitted. Neither could I ever willingly present myself to be kicked, as Shorty had done. I would rather have died than do that.

I could drain off my restlessness by fighting with Shorty and Harrison. I had seen many Negroes solve the problem of being black by transferring their hatred of themselves to others with a black skin and fighting them. I would have to be cold to do that, and I was not cold and I could never be.

I could, of course, forget what I had read, thrust the whites out of my mind, forget them; and find release from anxiety and longing in sex and alcohol. But the memory of how my father had conducted himself made that course repugnant. If I did not want others to violate my life, how could I voluntarily violate it myself?

I had no hope whatever of being a professional man. Not only had I been so conditioned that I did not desire it, but the fulfillment of such an ambition was beyond my capabilities. Well-to-do Negroes lived in a world that was almost as alien to me as the world inhabited by whites.

What, then, was there? I held my life in my mind, in my consciousness each day, feeling at times that I would stumble and drop it, spill it forever. My reading had created a vast sense of distance between me and the world in which I lived and tried to make a living, and that sense of distance was increasing each day. My days and nights were one long, quiet, continuously contained dream of terror, tension, and anxiety. I wondered how long I could bear it.

Richard Wright. *Black Boy: A Record of Childhood and Youth*. New York: Harper & Row Publishers, 1937, pp. 271–277.

Student B

He told no white men he was going north because then they would hate him. He was thinking of rebelling against the white men. But he didn't want to die. He hates the way negroes are mistreated and wants to change it.

He says he has no hope of being a professional man. I think that he is going to go crazy from all of the tension on his back.

Student A   **High**

The high score for Student A was based on the marginal notes that appear in the lefthand column that runs alongside the story, as well as the responses to questions 1–7, which follow. A summary commentary appears at the end of Student A's responses.

After You Have Read
Now that you have finished reading the selection, respond as fully as you can to the following seven questions and activities. You may refer to the reading selection as often as you like.

1. IDEAS: What is your response to the excerpt from this autobiography? Take a few minutes to write any thoughts, questions, or opinions you may have.

> **R u b r i c**
>
> **Rhetoric:** The writer directly engages with the subject matter of the story, connecting the text to personal knowledge.
>
> **Themes/Ideas:** The writer identifies a clear response to the story. The writer tells us his or her opinions and thoughts, including what he or she learned from the story. One of the central ideas of this assessment is the importance of books in growth and development.

> This autobiography made me realize, just how important books really are. I didn't know that negroes weren't allowed in libraries or that other people told blacks that books were bad for them.
>
> Reading this makes me want to learn more about black history and my history as well. I want to learn more about people and how they reacted in different situations in history. Learning that, will help me understand people today, and predict people's actions in the future.

Student A — High

2. **METAPHOR/LANGUAGE:** Choose one of the following quotations from the reading selection to write about. Explain what it might mean in the selection, what it means to you, how you feel about it, or any other comments you may have.

   A. "He was using words as weapons.... Could words be weapons?"
   B. "... I hungered for books, new ways of looking and seeing."

I am writing about the quotation labeled A

> Lashing out, cutting, punching; not a violent madman. No, just the words of a madman. Words can cut like a knife. Maybe they won't physically cut your flesh but they can scar your mind, your emotions and your heart.
>
> Sometimes harsh words are good and make you realize things. Other times they can just hurt and do nothing but make you think of unhappiness. Words can be as sweet as a flower or as deadly as a dagger.

R u b r i c

Rhetoric: The good writer appears to be answering a question from another reader.

Linguistics/Conventions: The writer has good control of language and conventions.

Themes/Ideas: The writer understands that the same words can be both threatening and helpful.

3. **COGNITION:** An "open mind" is an outline of a head that lets you show what a character might be thinking or feeling. In the "open mind" below use symbols, images, drawings, and/or words to show what Richard Wright might have been thinking or feeling in this excerpt from the autobiography.

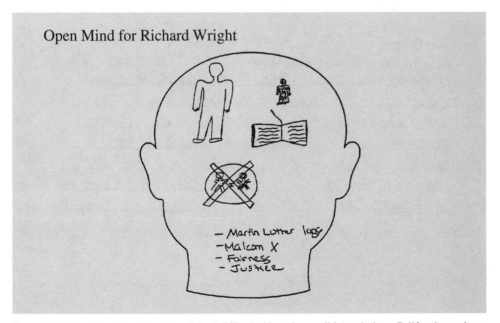

Open Mind for Richard Wright

— Martin Luther King
— Malcom X
— Fairness
— Justice

R u b r i c

Themes/Ideas: The writer presents a range of images, suggesting an awareness of what the author or character was thinking about.

NOTE: Most teachers found the Open Mind difficult (if not impossible) to judge. California teachers did *not* rank the prompts separately. They ranked them only together as one score. The Open Mind has been attacked as an imprecise and invasive device.

Student A   High

4. Explain how the symbols, images, drawings, and/or words you put into your "open mind" represent your ideas about Richard Wright.

R u b r i c

Cognition: The student is a fluent writer.
Rhetoric: These short-answer responses are difficult to judge as rhetorical samples.
Linguistics/Conventions: The writer has good command of language structures and conventions. There are a few missteps. The parallelism in the last sentence is impressive.
Themes/Ideas: The writer presents an accurate and rich description of the author's vision and goal.

> Richard Wright wrote about someone that we can all relate to. He's just a regular kid trying to make it in the world.
>
> This kid happens to want to know and learn more, but he knows that white men are imaged as bigger and stronger and negroes and other minorities are small and weak. They are just that minor. He also knows that him and his boss are unequal not only because his boss is higher on the corporate ladder, but because he's white

5. What were Richard Wright's reactions to the books he read?

R u b r i c

Themes/Ideas: The writer recognizes that books changed the author's understanding of the world.

> When Richard Wright read, he hungered to read even more. He realized his past and what his forefathers did for him. That made him want more for his life and want to move North. Reading made Wright understand.

Student A

6. At the end of the story, Richard Wright speculates about the kind of future he will choose to have. What do you think he will choose? Why do you think he will make these choices?

> At the end, Richard decides he wants to move north where life will still be hard for him. He will recieve pressuer from others as well as himself. By reading however, he will go stranger in his morals and values and not let himself be repressed.

R u b r i c

Cognition: The student appears to be a fluent writer and reader.
Themes/Ideas: The writer recognizes that Wright will move north and understands why he must do so.

7. This is your chance to tell anything else you want about your understanding of this autobiographical selection–what it means to you, what it reminds you of, how it relates to your own life, or whatever else you think is important about this reading selection.

> Autobiographies like the one that I just read are important for everyone. Every person needs to understand not only the people around him but the people before him too. Knowing about people of all different races and cultures helps you to live with eachother and not only tolerate others but love others as well.
> We all have a desire to seek and learn other peoples behaviors. We as humans and people on this earth have the responsibility to go out and learn about others and read.

R u b r i c

Cognition: The writer is fluent.
Rhetoric: The writer brings the reader into the explanation. The writer is aware that there is a reader who must be convinced.
Linguistics/Conventions: The writer has good control of conventions.
Themes/Ideas: The high writer understands how to use books to know things about the world.

Commentary for High Exemplar

This discerning, thorough, and perceptive reading performance shows a reader who has a clear understanding of the whole text as well as an awareness of how the parts work together to create the whole. This reader demonstrates an active engagement in the process of reading, connecting the text to his or her own ideas and experience as well as to the larger world.

Beginning with the margin notes, this student demonstrates a wide variety of reading performances. The reader clusters perceptive comments ("democracy everything human"), fills in gaps ("This person's life was sculpted by the white people around him"), speculates ("I thinks this boy's boss is a white man and has never even tried to relate to this black kid that works for him."), and personally connects to the text ("I wish I had the desire to read as many books as this person dose.") Throughout the margin notes this reader makes plausible, although not always insightful, assumptions about the text.

This reader sees connections between his or her life and the world of the text. In the initial response activity (Item 1) the reader articulates a personal insight and then connects that understanding to the historical community surrounding the text: "Reading this makes me want to learn more about black history and my history as well." The reader gives a few details to support this historical and cultural connection in Item 4 ("Martin Luther King, Malcolm X"). Additional personal connections are evident in the final response where the reader asserts ideas about the value of understanding "different races and cultures." While insightful, these comments tend to be more predictable than those of an exemplary performance.

In the graphic and the explanation of it, the reader continues to explore and expand his or her interpretation of the narrator's life: "Richard Wright wrote about someone that we can all relate to. He's just a regular kid trying to make it in the world. This kid happens to want to know and learn more. . . ." The reader concludes this assessment of the character by speculating that, by reading, Richard "Will go stronger in his morals and values and not let himself be repressed."

Low

Student B

The low score for Student B was based on the marginal notes that appear in the righthand column that runs alongside the story, as well as the responses to questions 1–7, which follow. A summary commentary appears at the end of the responses.

1. **IDEAS: What is your response to the excerpt from this autobiography? Take a few minutes to write any thoughts, questions, or opinions you may have.**

R u b r i c

Rhetoric: The writer does not engage with other readers of the book, presenting simple plot summaries as if they were opinions, concepts, or generative questions.

Themes/Ideas: The low writer often repeats what the narrator says. The writer's opinion seems to reflect a misunderstanding about what happened in the story.

I think that the negro really loves to read books and dreams of writing them someday. He thinks that the negroes are being mistreated and wants to rebel against them. I think he should move North and write novels and try to start a new life. I don't think he should have been so scared of the white men finding out about his reading books because he's not doing anything wrong.

Student B

2. METAPHOR/LANGUAGE: Choose one of the following quotations from the reading selection to write about. Explain what it might mean in the selection, what it means to you, how you feel about it, or any other comments you may have.

    A. "He was using words as weapons. . . . Could words be weapons?"

    B. ". . . I hungered for books, new ways of looking and seeing."

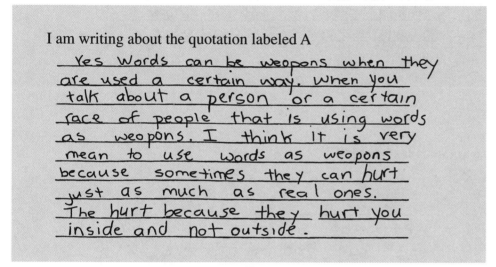

I am writing about the quotation labeled A

Yes words can be weapons when they are used a certain way. When you talk about a person or a certain race of people that is using words as weapons. I think It is very mean to use words as weapons because sometimes they can hurt just as much as real ones. The hurt because they hurt you inside and not outside.

R u b r i c

Rhetoric: The writer appears to address an inconsistent audience.

Linguistics/Conventions: The writer here and there loses control of language structure and conventions.

Themes/Ideas: The writer becomes focused about whether words are different from "real" weapons or whether words inflict "real" wounds. The resulting confusion about what to do with the question leads the writer to assert that talking about a person is using words as weapons.

3. COGNITION: An "open mind" is an outline of a head that lets you show what a character might be thinking or feeling. In the "open mind" below use symbols, images, drawings, and/or words to show what Richard Wright might have been thinking or feeling in this excerpt from the autobiography.

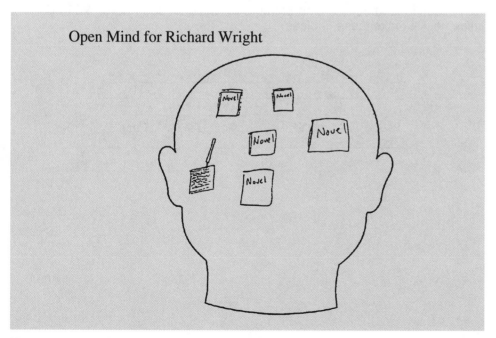

Open Mind for Richard Wright

R u b r i c

Themes/Ideas: The limited variation in images suggests a limited awareness of what was in the author's mind.

NOTE: Most teachers found the Open Mind difficult (if not impossible) to judge. California teachers did *not* rank the prompts separately. They ranked them only together as one score. The Open Mind has been attacked as an imprecise and invasive device.

Student B Low

4. Explain how the symbols, images, drawings, and/or words you put into your "open mind" represent your ideas about Richard Wright.

R u b r i c

Linguistics/Conventions: Very little text present, making any assessment of structure and conventions difficult.
Themes/Ideas: Underdeveloped, misleading assessment of the author's vision and goal.

> Richard Wright is only thinking about reading and writing novels That is what he really loves to do.

5. What were Richard Wright's reactions to the books he read?

R u b r i c

Themes/Ideas: The writer is vague about what books did for the author.

> Some of them made him feel good and some of them mad him feel bad and think the world was full of killing

6. At the end of the story, Richard Wright speculates about the kind of future he will choose to have. What do you think he will choose? Why do you think he will make these choices?

R u b r i c

Cognition: The student may not be a fluent writer or reader.
Themes/Ideas: The writer knows that Wright will move north but is vague about why he must do so.

> I think he will move to the North and write many really good books. I think he'll do that because thats the right thing to do.

Student B — Low

7. **This is your chance to tell anything else you want about your understanding of this autobiographical selection–what it means to you, what it reminds you of, how it relates to your own life, or whatever else you think is important about this reading selection.**

> I liked the autobiography selection a lot and I love to read really long books and hope to write them one day.

Rubric

Rhetoric: Uncertain relationship to reader.

Themes/Ideas: The writer is vague about the purposes of reading.

Commentary for Low Exemplar

Low performing readers characteristically construct literal, superficial interpretations of the text. This reader's margin notes are largely just that—literal and superficial renderings, opinions, and evaluations: "I think he is reading a book written by a very mean person. . . . He writes down exactly what he thinks . . . started to regard some of the other white men differently . . . tried to write a book . . . began saving money. . . ." Although these notes parallel the movement of the text, they show little sensitivity to the nuances and complexities that more proficient readers see in this text.

Occasionally this reader expresses a personal opinion that indicates that he or she is confident in his or her understanding, such as "I think that he is going crazy from all the tension on his back" or "I don't think he should have been so scared of the white men finding out about his reading books because he's not doing anything wrong." Although these opinions show some engagement with the text, they are largely superficial and unelaborated, showing little awareness of textual complexities.

This reader expresses his or her own connection to the text by saying "I like the autobiography selection a lot and I love to read really long books and hope to write them one day." This comment, along with the whole of the reader's responses, point to a reader who likes to read, who understands this text on a literal level, but who has not, in this assessment, demonstrated more than a superficial understanding of the passage. Once the student expressed a literal interpretation, he or she was content to retain this simplistic view without extending or expanding it, as is warranted by Wright's text.

Connections to Standards

	STANDARDS											
Targeted	1	2	3	4	5	6	7	8	9	10	11	12
Supplementary	1	2	3	4	5	6	7	8	9	10	11	12

This response-to-literature task targets students' skills at reading literature in depth (2) and invites them to apply a wide range of strategies, such as making marginal notes and using visual language, in order to comprehend, interpret, evaluate, and critique this text (3). If this task were embedded in a larger unit of classroom instruction, such as reading *Black Boy* in its entirety, students might explore the historical context of the work, as well as the social and cultural issues it raises (1). This particular text invites interdisciplinary connections and research on such topics as the 1920s, Jim Crow, and the Harlem Renaissance (7, 8). This text might also serve as a basis for study of issues of language, culture, and power (9). Students might compose, share, and publish various types of autobiographical writing in response to Wright's text (11, 12).

BREADTH OF READING

T a s k

To assess range of reading, teachers often ask students to keep a reading log showing their accomplishments. The students were asked to provide evidence that they had read:

- at least twenty-five books (or their equivalent in articles, newspapers, or textbooks) in the course of a year (knowing about);
- materials that are high quality, i.e., chosen from recognized reading lists (knowing about);
- a well-balanced selection of materials from classic and contemporary literature and from public discourse (documentary essays, news analyses, editorials) (knowing about);
- at least three different kinds (genres) of printed materials (e.g., novels, biographies, magazine articles) (knowing that);
- works of at least five different authors (knowing about);
- at least four books (or book equivalents) about one issue, or in one genre, or by a single author (or a combination of all of these) (knowing that).

NOTE: The first feature of the rubric is *twenty-five books* or the *equivalent.* This choice is obviously a big issue. What is an *equivalent?* Again, the answer is to be found in a combination of rubrics, commentaries, and samples at different levels of achievement. Finally, the rubric can be modified by asking students to write a brief explanation of how their booklists meet the requirements of the rubric. Students can explain, for instance, what recognized list they consulted.

Exemplar — High

R u b r i c

The reader meets all of the necessary requirements listed in the task (see above).

Books Tomes Novels TREASURES

The following list includes a selection of my favorite books that I've read during American Studies (An advanced placement class composed of History and English.) as well as on my own during the past year.

The Oedipus Plays of Sophocles, Sophocles
"Oedipus the King",
"Oedipus at Colonus",
"Antigone". -We as a nation a very concerned with family values today, and often want to return to the "old days." Wouldn't Oedipus and his family give us an extremely unpleasant suprise!
The Giver, Lois Lowry-For Jonas and his family, life is perfect...but where is it taking them?!?!
The Scarlet Letter, Nathaniel Hawthorne-"A" is for adultery, as well as agony, angellic and anaclitic.
Rappaccini's Daughter, Nathaniel Hawthorne-Rappaccini was torn between the love he felt for his daughter and his beloved plants.
Come Spring, Ben Ames Williams-Life was not easy in the backwoods of Maine in the late 1700's. They were rich in family, faith, and in the hope of the coming spring.
Brave New World, Aldous Huxely-Life is wonderful...as long as it feels that way!
Heart of Darkness, Joseph Conrad-We never know what will change with the weather, in the jungles of inner Africa.
The Secret Sharer, Joseph Conrad-Relationships form, like two ships colliding in the night.
Night, Elie Wiesel-Life must go on with visions of burning babies and rooms of death. Always remember...never forget!
Damian, Hermann Hesse-The sky is the limit for those who find spirituality in themselves.

40

Siddhertha, Hermann Hesse-IF the Buddah is truly divine, then friendship must be his master.
Steppenwolf, Hermann Hesse-Terror is nothing to be afraid of..until it looks you in the face.
The Tempest, William Shakespeare-The fantasy based on the colonization of America. Shall Prospero choose love over vengeance?
The Taming of the Shrew, William Shakespeare-IF you think Katharine is a shrew...meet Bianca!
Twelfth Night, William Shakespeare-Poor Malvolio, learn a lesson from Viola and Sebastian.
Macbeth, William Shakespeare-By the twitching of my thumbs; something wicked this way comes. Something WICKED this way comes!
Immortal Wife, Irving Stone, John C. Fremont conquered the west, his wife placed him on a petiestal.
Those Who Love, Irving Stone, John and Abigail Adams were married in law and patriotism.
The President's Lady, Irving Stone, Oh, in 1814 we took a little trip, along with Andrew Jackson down the mighty Mississipp...
Cold Sassy Tree, Olive Ann Burns, Everyone felt sorry for Grandpa after Grandma died...until he brought home his new wife! News travels fast in Alabama.
Hopkins of the Mayflower, Margaret Hodges, The story of a man who wanted more, and achieved it.
Constance, Patricia Clapp. Life was hard in early Plymouth, but life is always hard when you're fourteen.
Arundel, Kenneth Roberts, Life was dull for Steven...until Benedict Arnold came along!
Frankenstein, Mary Shelley, Victor had created a monster...inside himself!
Walden, Henry David Thoreau-Lay back in a rowboat and let yourself drift...
Volatile Truths, Martin Bickman-A story of Thoreau's *Walden*, and what inspired him.
Spoon River Anthology, Edgar Lee Masters-All, all are sleeping, sleeping on the hill.
Silas Marner, Silas Marner-Silas is a miser even without his gold, until a child appeared.
The Client, John Grisham-The mob is always listening!
Midnight in the Garden of Good and Evil, John Berendt, Savannah is a beautiful town...until skeletons start falling out of closets...literally!
Seed of Sarah, Judith Isaacson-The courageous story of a young Jewish girl trying to survive in Nazi prison and death camps.
Suivez la Piste, Emile de Harven-Fait attention le virus dangereux!
Un Bouquet, Hermin Dubus-Monologues et d'a propos pur toutes les fetes de l'annee.
Le Fantome de l'Opera, Gaston Leroux-L'histoire triste d'un homme, a demi monstre et a demi enfant.
24 Favorite One-Act Plays,
"27 Wagons Full of Cotten"-Tennessee Williams
"Spreading the News"-Lady Gregory
"A Marriage Proposal"-Anton Chekhov
"In the Shadow on the Glen"-J.M. Synge
"Cathleen ni Houlihan"-W.B. Yeats
"The Jest of Hahalaba"-Lord Dunsany
"Trifles"-Susan Glaspell
"The Happy Journey"-Thornton Wilder
"The Ugly Duckling"-A.A. Milne
"The Flattering Word"-George Kelly
"The Tridget of Greve"-Ring Lardner
"The Moon of the Caribbees"-Eugene O'Neil
"The Still Alarm"-George S. Kaufman
"The Devil and Daniel Webster"-Stephen Vincent Benet
"The Apollo of Bellac"-Jean Giraudoux
"A Memory of Two Mondays"-Arthur Miller
"Glory in the Flower"-William Inge
"Hands Across the Sea"-Noel Coward
"Here We Are"-Dorothy Parker
"Sorry, Wrong Number"-Lucille Fletcher
"The Browning Version"-Terence Rettigan
"A Florentine Tragedy"-Oscar Wilde
"The Maker of Dreams"-Oliphant Down
"The Traveler"-Marc Connelly
This Same Sky, Compiled by Naomi Shihab Nye-a collection of poems from around the world.

Commentary

This student has documented a prodigious amount of reading, exceeding the requirement of twenty-five books or book equivalents. The works listed are both high quality and challenging. The works listed represent a well-balanced selection of materials from classic (e.g., *The Oedipus Plays of Sophocles*) and contemporary literature (e.g., *Cold Sassy Tree*). Little, if any, reading in public discourse is documented here. This is a serious shortcoming which needs to be corrected. The student has read at least three different kinds of printed materials, including novels, short stories, poetry, and drama. The student has read the works of considerably more than five different writers and has read in depth in the areas of historical fiction, utopian literature, and drama.

The succinct and sometimes provocative comments about each work listed (e.g., "Wouldn't Oedipus and his family give us an extremely unpleasant surprise!") suggest that the student has engaged with the texts listed. Other notable features of this student's reading include several works read in French and a good balance of U.S. and world literature. This avid reader would probably benefit from reading more nonfiction texts and more literature of the diverse cultures of the United States. The four books on one issue could be the four plays by Shakespeare or the books related in some way to *Walden*. The student has an excellent list, but the student needs to be explicit about *how* the list meets the different requirements. Good work is only one of the challenges to each student. The other challenge is to present clearly the re-lationships between one's achievement and the standards outlined in the task.

Exemplar   Middle

Rubric

The reader falls below the requirements for high achievement listed in the task. Middle readers tend to read ten to fifteen books and to limit the range.

Commentary

This student has documented a moderate amount of reading, including about six complete books. Several entries on the reading list consist of very short texts, e.g., "To a Mouse," an encyclopedia article, and various readings in popular magazines and newspapers. Except for sports materials, the student has not concentrated on one issue. Most of the works listed are adequate selections. The works listed represent a fairly limited range of classic and contemporary literature. The range of nonfiction reading—in *Sports Illustrated, Reader's Digest,* and newspapers—is somewhat limited as well. Thus, limited reading of public discourse is documented here.

The student has read in at least three different genres, e.g., poems, a drama, novels, but the quality of the reading is questionable. Similarly, the student has read at least five different authors, meeting the letter but not the spirit of the task. The student has read three novels in the fantasy genre, falling short of the number required by the task. On the portfolio entry slip for his reading list, this student wrote that he had met his goal of reading in a "bigger variety of genres. . . . Now, I just have to start reading more!"

12/13

TITLE	AUTHOR	GENRE	PAGES
Druid of Shannara	Terry Brooks	Novel	423 pgs.
National Geographic	William Garret	Non-Fiction	10 pgs.
Reader's Digest	Various	Short-Stories	30 pgs.
Of Mice & Men	Steinbeck	Novel	118 pgs.
To a Mouse	Robert Burns	Poetry	1 pg.
Sports Illustrated	Various	Magazine	30 pgs.
A Seperate Peace	John Knowles	Novel	196 pgs.
Sports Section News	Various	Newspaper	20 pgs.
Matter & Energy	Unknown-	Scientific	2 pgs.
Story of Robert Hook	Encyclopedia	Biography	2-3 pgs.
Princess Bride	Robert Goldman ??	Novel	200+ pgs.
My Crazy Life	Luis Rodriguez	Novel Auto-Biography	200 pgs.
Talismans of Shanarra	Terry Brooks	Novel	453 pgs.
Sports Section	Various	Newspaper	30 pgs.
Computer Articles (Gangs)	Various	Articles	20 pgs.
Our Town	Thorton Wilder	Play	30 pgs (?)
Poem Packet	Various	Poetry	6 poems
Robert Frost Anthology	Robert Frost	Poetry	2 poems
Readers Digest	Various	Short-Stories	25 pgs.
LIFE: Italy	Unknown	History	15 pgs.

R u b r i c

The low reader either reads very little, zero to ten books, or else reads twenty pieces which are of uncertain quality and uncertain form. The low reader may not be a fluent reader.

```
                     BOOK LIST

    I have read the following books this year:

    1:     THE HAUNTED ONE by Bennett
    2:     SKINHEAD by Bennett
    3:     THEY CAGE THE ANIMALS AT NIGHT by Burch
    4:     OF MICE AND MEN by John Steinbeck
    5:     CALL WAITING by Stine
    6:     THE FACE ON THE MILK CARTON by Cooney
    7:     WHATEVER HAPPENED TO JANIE? by Cooney
    8:     TEACHER PET by Cusick
    9:     THAT WAS THEN AND THIS IS NOW by Hinton
    10:    HIT AND RUN by Stine
```

Commentary

This student has documented reading ten short novels and, given the demands of these ten books, the student has fallen short of the requirement of twenty-five or more. All the works listed are fiction, including one classic novel, *Of Mice and Men,* and several adolescent classics, e.g., *That Was Then and This Is Now*. The works of five different authors are represented on this list. There is no evidence that the student has read in depth on any of the dimensions described in the task. For example, the student does not attempt a balance of contemporary and classic texts or a focus on four books on one issue or by one author. The student does have at least four in one genre. This student appears to have the basics under control, and now needs to concentrate on expanding range and increasing depth.

NOTE: The teachers who experimented with ways of collecting evidence on Breadth of Reading and then ranked that evidence have generally concluded that students need an example format for describing the books they read. The format should include: (1) full title; (2) complete name of author; (3) number of pages; (4) genre; (5) central theme; (6) one-sentence plot summary; and (7) one-sentence evaluation. At the end, the student should describe how the list meets the task requirements.

Connections to Standards

	STANDARDS											
Targeted	1	2	3	4	5	6	7	8	9	10	11	12
Supplementary	1	2	3	4	5	6	7	8	9	10	11	12

This task challenges students to read a wide range of texts, both literary and nonliterary (1, 2). If more extensive documentation were required, students might also demonstrate the knowledge, skills, and strategies they use when reading (3, 6). This task might also be structured to require reading works which help students develop an understanding of and respect for diversity (9). Students should be encouraged to document reading done to accomplish their own purposes (12).

Portfolios

The section that follows contains excerpts from the portfolios of three high school students—Natalie, Loretta, and Terry. From each portfolio we have selected only a few pieces for inclusion here. In some cases, we show only excerpts of pieces, but enough to give you a general idea of the quality of the whole piece. The purpose of this section is to give you an idea of what a collection of a student's work—as opposed to a single sample—may reveal about that student's learning and accomplishments in English language arts.

The selections from Natalie's, Loretta's, and Terry's portfolios represent a range of levels of performance—high (Natalie), middle (Loretta), and low (Terry). We are not suggesting that Natalie's work represents the very best that has been or could ever be done. Likewise, we are not suggesting that Terry's work represents some absolute minimum level. Our intent is to represent some of the range of performances which English teachers encounter in today's heterogeneously grouped classes and to represent the judgments which teachers make about the levels of achievement in those performances, using the *Standards for the English Language Arts* (NCTE/IRA).

Natalie, Loretta, and Terry are students in different classrooms from different parts of the country. When they assembled their portfolios, they were participating in the second year of the field trial of the New Standards English language arts portfolio system,[1] which was at that time managed by the Literacy Unit at NCTE. This system requires students to show examples of their best work and to follow a common "menu" in putting together their portfolios. This menu was based on the NCTE/IRA standards. Among the required items were

- evidence of reading accomplishment in literature, informational materials, and public discourse;
- evidence of quantity, range, and depth in reading;
- evidence of writing in a variety of genres or modes (e.g., argument or persuasion, narration, report of information);
- evidence of speaking, listening, and viewing;
- an introductory reflective essay describing what the contents of the portfolio suggest about growth in English language arts;
- a table of contents.

Natalie's, Loretta's, and Terry's portfolios were scored by teachers in their local states and districts, and then sent to a national meeting, where they were scored by teachers from across the country. Many of these portfolios were scored again by NCTE teachers in NCTE's national meetings. Some of these teachers' judgments and comments appear in the rubric-based marginal comments and the summary commentaries at the end of each portfolio. For the sake of simplicity, rubrics and commentaries are combined into one for each entry. The summaries discuss the degree to which the portfolio as a whole represents achievement in the three ways of knowing (i.e., knowing that, knowing how, knowing about), the four domains of English language arts described in the introduction to this book (i.e., cognition, rhetoric, linguistics/conventions, and cultural themes or ideas), and the six activities or forms of representation of English classes (i.e., reading, writing, speaking, listening, viewing, and representing).

Throughout this section, "Connections to Standards," which appear in the margins, show connections between relevant portions of the NCTE/IRA standards and individual entries. These are not the *only* possible connections that could be made between the standards and the portfolio entries; they are, however, particularly salient connections.

The work that you see here will undoubtedly prompt you to ask many questions about the work itself and about the circumstances leading to and surrounding the production of the final portfolio. We hope that you will pursue these questions with your colleagues and that you will understand that we cannot address here all the provocative issues raised when we study, interpret, and evaluate student work.

---

[1] New Standards is a partnership of approximately twenty states and urban districts working to build an assessment system that measures students' progress toward achieving a set of standards (also being developed by New Standards).

Portfolios

Natalie

Loretta

Terry

Natalie compiled this portfolio at the end of her eleventh-grade year. Her portfolio represents a selection of the work she completed over the course of the school year. We have selected only a few pieces for inclusion here. Some of the pieces are excerpts only.

Note: The letters in the rubrics/commentaries should be matched with the letters in the margins of the student work, thereby showing the location of the features cited.

Task

Natalie chose to include a cover with her portfolio.

A.

B.

C.

This Above All; To Thine Own Self Be True

William Shakespeare

Rubric / Commentary

A. The title page is effectively designed and attractive to audience.
B. Shakespearean quote establishes theme which is maintained throughout the portfolio.
C. Quote engages reader's interest in this portfolio.

Reflective Essay (Letter)

High

Task

Following are excerpts from Natalie's reflective essay. The whole essay is written in the form of a letter addressed to the portfolio reader and interweaves quotations from Shakespeare, the poetry of Robert Frost, and personal anecdotes to create a portrait of Natalie as a "reader, writer and learner."

Rubric / Commentary

A. Engages the reader by direct address and sets context for personal background which follows.

B. Continues Shakespearean theme from cover in reflective essay.

C. Explains significance of portfolio title. Natalie is trying out ideas, and we celebrate her efforts. She sees herself as getting serious.

D. Introduces self as reader and establishes goal for reading.

E. Natalie is beginning, she says, to think about her own learning and thinking. She is clearly fluent in the basics and is moving to a more conscious reflection about her work.

F. Shows awareness of growth in reading. Identifies specific works read and why they were enjoyable, making a personal connection.

Hey Nonny,

A. Before I begin, it is important that you, the reader, understand a few things about me. In the past English classes, the curriculum has included a unit of Shakespeare study. I never **B.** truly appreciated the language until this year. Comprehension of the language happened gradually. I became frustrated because I'd never given Shakespeare half a chance. This year, when we read <u>Hamlet</u>, I kept an open mind and worked hard to stay focused. The more we read, the easier it became to understand.

During the year, one of the greatest lessons I've learned has come through my experiences with Shakespeare. After deep contemplation, I've realized that no better advice could ever be **C.** given to a person than the counsel which Polonius gave to his daughter. "This above all: to thine own self be true." . . . .

I've worked hard for the ability to stay focused on life and on aspiring to do well in school…especially English class. There will be times when I won't always choose the right path…learning to live with my decisions is a goal I've set for myself. This isn't the only goal I'm aiming for…there are many, many more.

In the future, I wish to continue reading a wide variety of **D.** literature as I've done throughout the school year. In the past, my parents and teachers have always encouraged me to read and I have done so with sincere ardor. Losing myself in the pages of a book and blocking out hassles of daily life is an important part **E.** of my weekly routine.

Until this year, I was still reading silly mystery books by R. L. Stine and Christopher Pike. This was partially because I'd never really been introduced to any other mystery authors. My teacher suggested I read a Mary Higgins Clark book and I did **F.** just that…all in the same night. I fell in love with these stories and whenever I pick one up, the book usually doesn't get put down until it is finished.

G. Natalie is beginning to see herself as a writer and reviews her accomplishments.
H. As a reader and writer, she develops strong connections between the general and the specific.
I. Identifies specific pieces that show growth in writing.
J. Connects importance of broad vocabulary to both reading and writing.

At the beginning of the year, I never thought I would ever actually read a classic novel in my free time. For class, we were all required to read a classic and do a text reaction. Later on, I found myself reading another classic, and then another…all during my free time. One novel I especially enjoyed was <u>The Moonstone</u> by Wilkie Collins. It was a complicated mystery with a twisted ending…one I never would've guessed in a million years. That's what made it so great. The author kept my attention throughout the text. Inside and outside of class this year, I managed to read about thirty books…everyone of them appealed to me in one way or another. Recently, I became interested in poetry and have been reading selections by Robert Frost.

G. This year, I have done a lot of creative writing, composing many short stories and imaginative papers for English class. I feel the more I write, the better the finished pieces are. Just as the famous quote says, "Practice makes perfect." After re-reading past writings, I can see major contrasts with my current
H. writings. The sentence structures are now more complete with more appropriate dialect and correct word placement. I have realized that adjective placement within a paragraph is so important. To me, it means either a phrase which flows well, or one that sounds choppy and incomplete. Taking the time to sit down and work with a rough draft is something I've been working with all year. One piece which I believe is a good example of this is my critical analysis paper. My points were out of order and with
I. suggestions from my teacher, I cut them out and pasted them back together in a more logical order.

I have begun to realize how important a good vocabulary is. Whenever I come upon a word I am unfamiliar with, I reach for
J. my dictionary and find the meaning. I have myself groping for words to fill the empty spaces. It's hard not to sound repetitive at times and with a more imaginative vocabulary, this wouldn't always be a problem.

One of my strengths in writing is selecting a theme from a book and expanding on it. This is done by using effective quotes to prove a point or solve the problem I've discovered. I get very involved when doing research for such projects and lose all sense

Paper continued on page 50

K. Cites specific weakness and states possible strategy to overcome it. This is an important developmental transition for Natalie. Her self-awareness is commendable.

L. Restates purpose of this portfolio and reviews accomplishments of past year.

M. Restates portfolio theme and alludes to newly discovered pleasure in Frost's poetry.

N. Concludes with a personal wish for the portfolio reader and closes courteously and appropriately.

O. She has excellent control of conventions throughout.

Connections to Standards

Natalie demonstrates substantial achievement in:

• participating as a knowledgeable, reflective, creative, and critical member of a literacy community (11).

of time, but not direction. I possess the ability to stay focused on the assigned task and it comes in handy when I have a lot of work to do.

Throughout the year, I have been trying to use a more colorful vocabulary to heighten the flavor of my writing. This is an aspect I will continue to work on for the rest of my life. Imagination and figurative language help make a paper what it is.

K. One weakness I plan to work on is the development of many types of moods. Usually, when I write, the mood is peaceful and calm, but life doesn't always work that way. I need to learn to create a setting where the reader can feel the tension mounting or the fear running through the victim's body. Choosing to compose a wider genre of writings should help me accomplish this goal.

L. The portfolio I've assembled is one which represents me very well as reader, writer and learner. The goals I set for myself at the beginning of the year have been attained. My main obsta-

M. cle I wanted to conquer was to write in a more mature manner...I feel I've accomplished this goal. I am very proud of myself for all the hours of hard work and dedication I have put into this representation of me. I have heeded Polonius' and Frost's words...above all I have been true to myself and taken the road less traveled by. I have celebrated learning and that has made all

N. the difference. I hope you enjoy living the experience of my

O. portfolio.

Thank you,

Task

Natalie's entry slip states that the assignment was to "choose a controversial topic and defend one side of it." Students were required to "create a thesis statement," generate a "list of pros and cons," and "research the background" of the topic. Students then presented their research to the class. The entry slip states that this piece was "written for a wide range of audiences . . . people I know and those I don't . . . an informed reader and the un-informed reader."

Argument

High

WRITING TO PERSUADE

Persuasive Speech: Women In Baseball

Thesis: A woman who has the inspiration and possesses necessary talents should play on a Major League Baseball Team if she survives the tryout.

Women in Baseball

A. "All right folks, this is it. The Sox are down to their last batter. It's the bottom of the ninth, bases loaded, two outs and they're down by one…can they do it? Things are looking mighty good. Striding to the plate is Big Bad Mitchell. Leads the majors in nearly every offensive category! Now there's something to be reckoned with…45 homeruns, 130 RBI's and a seasonal batting average of .400.

   Glavine's conferring with his catcher on the situation. As far as I'm concerned, the only option they have is to pitch to the

B. batter…an intentional walk would tie the game. Mitchell's setting up in the batter's box. The homeplate umpire breaks up the meeting on the mound. Intensity is mounting here at Fenway Park and there is much speculation whether or not Mitchell can save the World Series.

   Glavine goes into his wind-up and the ball hums toward the plate, breaking at the last minute…Mitchell watches it sail past. "Strike one!" What is Mitchell thinking! That was a meatball! We should be watching that ball fly over the fence right now…not sitting here with our jaws drooping in shock.

   Glavine winds-up, the deliver…"Strike two!" What is Mitchell doing?! How much money did that strike have riding on it. Everyone go home…game over. Mitchell's throwing the pennant away.

Paper continued on page 52

C. Creates effective surprise ending to anecdote by revealing the batter's sex.

D. The strength of the opening narrative almost overwhelms the argumentative discourse which follows.

E. Strongly states own position in efficiently constructed thesis paragraph. The paragraph contains an overview of paper's major points.

F. The writer has good command of conventions. But there are a few missteps which could be easily fixed by a rereading or with an editing group. The writer's fluency is commendable.

G. Supports claim with example from current events.

C.

D.

Mitchell steps out of the batter's box and takes a quick glance at the pitcher. Glavine wipes the sweat from his brow. Everyone is set. Glavine checks the runners, sets himself and fires. The ball floats towards home. Without an effort in the world, Mitchell takes a step toward the pitcher, extends the bat and sends a rope towards left field. It's going, going, it is gone. Alice Mitchell has done it! She's won the World Series for the Red Sox! It's a new world record. She's the first woman MVP of the World Series."

E.

These are the words I would like to hear coming from an announcers mouth in the future. Women have been kept down for too long and it is time for them to display their talents and live their dreams. A woman who has the inspiration and possesses necessary talents should play on a Major League Baseball team if she survives the tryout. There are many women who are capable of playing baseball with the men, the only thing holding them back is a great discrimination barrier. There is this stereotype that women are just not up to par with the men, but a woman can work just as hard as a man to be successful at the sport. In the past, women have proved themselves capable of playing professional ball. A woman can adjust to the dimensions of the field and adjust to other tools needed for baseball play.

F.

Women in baseball seems to be a popular idea for the future of the sport.

G.

In the United States, there are many women who are capable of playing professional ball. Their talents to play the game seem to go unnoticed for the majority of the time. Recently, two women from the Colorado Silver Bullets (an all women's team) had a tryout with the New York Mets. These women received a fair tryout and were judged by the same standards as the men were. They went through the same running and throwing drills as the men and were not judged any easier because they were women. John Barr, director of scouting for the Mets, said gender had nothing to do with it. The two women were being looked at as numbers just like everyone else…they were not being discriminated against because of their sex.

Women should not be discriminated against because of their sex. They should be given a fair chance and not have to face slanders for their efforts. In the past, women have put their heart

H. and soul into living their dreams and often times, in order to live their dreams, they were heavily exploited and discriminated. A woman's place was in the home and that was that. "They thought it was a violation of the male environment." Playing baseball was totally rebellious and morally wrong and if you did such a thing you were looked down upon, that is unless you were young and beautiful and didn't mind breaking a nail now and then. "On August 26, 1890, a New York gentleman named W.S.

I. Franklin announced his intention to form a Women's Professional Baseball League. His advertisement read, 1890: Wanted: One Sexy Shortstop…must be young, not over 20, good looking and good figure." Applicants outside of the city were requested to send photographs." The point of this league was not to promote baseball, but to promote sex and make money. Women of the All-American Girls Professional Baseball League were forced to wear skirts as uniforms. This not only hindered their performance, it took away their self-respect. These women had to work twice as hard to prove to the world they were capable of playing baseball and they weren't just a sideshow in a circus. Despite all the criticism these women faced, they proved themselves capable of playing a man's sport.

In the past, women have proved themselves capable of playing baseball. In 1943, the All-American Girls Professional Baseball League was formed by P.K. Wrigley in Chicago. Baseball players were being drafted to go overseas and fight in the war…it was their patriotic duty. No one wanted to shut down the American past-time. President Franklin D. Roosevelt felt the same way. "People will be working longer hours and

J. working harder than before and they ought to have a chance for recreation and taking their minds off work." So scouts were sent out to look for young women to form this new league. . . . .

A woman can adjust to the dimensions of a baseball field and adjust to the tools necessary to play baseball. These tools being bat size, ball size, homerun distance, distance between the bases and pitching distance. The dimensions of a baseball field are closely proportional to the dimensions of a softball field. The factors involved with each sport make it seem as though women are incapable of playing baseball. The first thing that needs to be looked at is the ball and bat size. A softball is approximately 12

K. inches in diameter and weighs about 6 ounces compared to a 9 inch diameter baseball which weighs 5 ounces. The softball bat

H. Supports claim with historical anecdote.

I. Does the quotation (") start at "On August 26 . . ." or at "Wanted . . ."? The quotation after "photographs" does not seem appropriate.

J. Supports claim with historical evidence and quotes authority, Franklin Roosevelt.

K. Supports claim by demonstrating knowledge of technical elements of baseball.

53

Paper continued on page 54

L. Cites specific dimensions to enhance authority.

M. Continues to demonstrate technical knowledge.

N. The writer presents a substantial amount of information in concise, easily read prose. She has an excellent sense of sentence structure.

O. Cites results of survey she took to determine other students' attitudes toward topic.

P. Personal voice reemerges in final paragraph. Recapitulates thesis and concludes with a call for action.

NOTE: Natalie's audiotape of the oral presentation of her argument is not included here. On this tape, Natalie included realistic sound effects from an actual baseball game and argued her case with confidence and conviction.

Connections to Standards

Natalie demonstrates substantial achievement in:

• using writing to communicate effectively with a particular audience for a specific purpose (4);

• applying knowledge of language structure and language conventions to create a written text (6);

• conducting research on an issue of interest and communicating discoveries in ways that suit her purpose and audience (7).

L. is restricted to a maximum of 34 inches in length, against 42 inches of a baseball bat. The diameter of a softball bat may not exceed 2 1/4 inches as against baseball's 2 3/4 inches. When batted, a softball does not consistently travel as fast nor as far as a baseball, hence the shorter homerun distances for a softball field.

M. The larger ball may give the impression that a batter can get a better hit...the opposite is true. The bat is narrower and unless the batter hits the ball squarely in the center, a pop-up or a weak dribbler may result.

The shorter distance between the bases makes it easier for runners to advance. This is why a base runner is not allowed to take a lead until the pitcher releases the ball. The longer distances between baseball basepaths give the runners the advantage to take leads and get a good jump on the pitch.

One last major point, the softball pitcher is 46 feet from the batter, the baseball pitcher 60 1/2 feet. People facing softball pitchers have relatively the same reaction time that baseball players do when facing a baseball pitcher. The longer distance

N. between the mounds accounts for the reaction time players of both games have. Women would be able to adjust to these new dimensions because like it or not, they have been facing them all their life...all that is required is a little experience. People realize this and they understand that with experience, women can play baseball as well as the men. Women in baseball was a popular idea according to the results of my survey. 95% of those

O. surveyed would like to see women playing Major League Baseball in the future. Some interesting comments I received were as follows..."Men think they are better sport's players, it's time to show them women can play just as good, maybe even better than they can!" "It might actually be more fun to watch (meaning women playing baseball) then watching tobacco chewing guys grabbing their crotches."

In my opinion, if a women wants to play baseball than she should have every right to...without having to face discrimination. These walls need to be torn down in order for women to

P. feel comfortable playing in a male dominated sport. If she has the talents to play on the team, these talents should be praised just as everyone else's talents are praised and not criticized. The talent is there. It is time for some cooperation between the men and the women.

Task

Students were asked to include notes used in preparing the arguments. Notice which points actually appear in Natalie's final paper.

with the necessary talent women should have a fair tryout without being discriminated against and if they're good though, play on a MLB team!

College English III

Persuasive Speech Thesis

Thesis: **Women should be given the opportunity to play** Major League Baseball.

Cons

*women are wimps
*women don't have the knowledge or experience
*women should stick to softball
*couldn't handle hitting the pitching
*allowing women to play would break the tradition of men
    only
*women aren't used to the dimensions of the field and could
    never adjust
*women are incapable of hitting the ball out of the park
*women would be a disgrace to the game

Pros

*women are just as capable as men to play the sport
*not allowing women to play is sex discrimination
*with practice, women's baseball skills could be as good as
    the men's
*softball pitching is as complex as baseball pitching
*women should have equal rights and opportunities
*women can work as hard as men to be successful at baseball
*a) 90 MPH fastball will hurt a man just as much as it would
    hurt a women
*women can recover from injuries just as fast as men
*the men might learn a thing or two

women are now starting in NHL

there are women who are capable of playing the spa

women can work as hard as men to be successful

The dimensions of the field, size of ball, bat siz pitching distance make women appear

uncabable of playing baseball

This is not true. Go to homeruns, reaction time. ball size, bats.

a 90 MPH fastball will hurt a man just as much as it will hurt a women.

Commentary

Natalie uses writing to think about
    and plan her paper. She is willing
    to scratch notes and repeat herself
    when necessary.
Almost all of these details find their
    way into her paper, showing that
    her use of exploratory notes was
    not superficial.

Connections to Standards

Natalie demonstrates substantial achievement in:

● using different elements of the writing process appropriately (5).

Commentary

Natalie also included research notes in which she uses sketching to represent dimensions of playing fields.

The combination of visuals and writing is common in exploratory notes.

Connections to Standards

Natalie demonstrates substantial achievement in:

• applying a wide range of strategies to comprehend and interpret texts (3);

• employing a wide range of strategies as she writes (5).

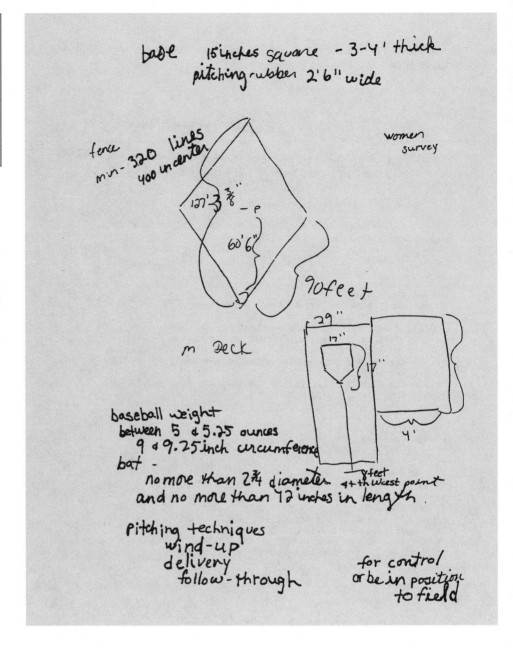

Task

Natalie included in her portfolio a copy of the survey she used as part of her research process.

Women in Baseball

Please feel free to make any comments in the space provided.

1. If a women has the necessary baseball skills, do you believe she should play on a Major League team.

2. Do you believe it is fair for teams such as the Colorado Silver Bullets (an all womens baseball team) to compete against MLB teams who have had many years of experience?

3. Do you believe women should to have their own baseball organizations such as there was from 1943-1954 called the All-American Girls Professional Baseball League?

4. Would you like to see women playing Major League Baseball in the future?

Commentary

Natalie prepared a survey to elicit quotations which she could use in her argument. Some of the questions seem to overlap a great deal (1 and 2), but Natalie's use of the survey enriched her resources for her argument.

Connections to Standards

Natalie demonstrates substantial achievement in:

• gathering data from a variety of sources (7).

Task

On the entry slip for this piece, Natalie states that it began as an autobiographical journal entry. She was so pleased with this entry that, after numerous rewrites, she submitted it for publication in the high school newspaper as her commentary on her response to a public issue. The published version appears below.

Rubric/Commentary

A. With the title, Natalie recalls her Shakespearean theme.

B. Natalie espouses a position that may not be very popular among this newspaper's readership—a fact she acknowledges in the final paragraph.

C. She states her position clearly in the first paragraph, ending with a question.

D. She answers the question by describing her own experience and the moment at which she realized the importance of doing well in school.

E. She concludes by briefly stating some lessons she has learned from school.

Connections to Standards

Natalie demonstrates substantial achievement in:

• using writing to communicate effectively with a particular audience for a specific purpose (4);

• using writing to accomplish her own purposes (12).

The 21st Century

To Achieve or Not to Achieve

A. *"Academic excellence. It used to be a goal so treasured that nearly everyone aspired to achieve it. Today, it seems, it is all but ignored."*— Keynote Speaker Cindy Elflein Jagord

B. When I walk down the halls of school each day it is not uncommon for me to hear comments concerning students' dislike for school.

C. Shocked is not the word I would use to describe my feelings . . . pity works better. For me, school is my second home which I love very much. Sometimes it is difficult for me to under-

D. stand why people feel this way. School is too important to be taken lightly. It is our duty to go to school and learn to the best of our ability so when we get out into the business world we will be well prepared. School is much easier for me to live with because I love it.

E. There is so much compassion inside of me for the

world that I want everyone to have as much fun as I do. We are given the opportunities to make the grade and aim high. So then my question is why do people settle for average when they can strive for excellence?

During my high school years, I've sometimes gotten caught up with the whole attitude . . . school's not cool. My grades have always been above average, but there have been times when I just didn't care anymore. Getting good grades came naturally so I never put much effort into my classes. At the end of freshman year, we received our report cards and I was very surprised when I saw I was sixth in my class. Something in me snapped and I realized school was no longer a joke. My grades were very good and I should be proud. I'd always taken school for

granted and now, I had an incentive to work hard and try to go up in my class ranking. That has made all of the difference. Since that day, I've been working hard to strive for excellence and have strayed from the crowd because I know school is cool. That's my opinion!

I now strive for academic excellence and it is a goal I set for myself. School has had a positive influence on my life and has taught me a very important lesson. It is a quote ____ has on the front of her desk. "What is popular is not always right; what is right is not always popular." School has taught me it isn't always important to follow the crowd, there are times when you have to be a trailblazer and lead the way . . . be a positive influence and let others follow you. It's time to stick up for myself and be proud of my grades . . . they are the things that will get me far in life. ●

Task

Natalie described the assignment as follows: "The assignment was to choose a piece of literature we are familiar with and create a thesis statement from a topic from the book. Then we were to write a dialectical journal, using quotes we would include within our paper. In this piece, we were to discuss the thesis statement using situations from the book and from the world. We were also to create a probable solution for the problem at hand." Natalie selected Virginia Woolf's *Mrs. Dalloway.*

Response to Literature

High

Commentary

This is an excerpt from the entry slip which accompanied this piece. Here Natalie reveals some of the strategies she used in reading the novel and outlines how her intentions evolved in this piece of writing.

This book was written in stream of thought. This was frustrating, but I kept chipping away at it. I read the book nearly 3 times to be familiar with the text...inside and out. The stream of thought jumped from character to character so quickly I often got lost, so I went back and reread the passage 'til I understood it completely. The points in my piece are set up very logically with good support to back them up. A hook begins the piece and is referred to at the end, wrapping the paper into completion. This paper was actual events from daily living in relation to a major theme from the book. This is a very serious paper and is not meant to be taken lightly. Some time form contemplation of what has been written needs to be taken to truly analyze where the world is headed...something needs to be done.

Rubric / Commentary

A. Identifies and explores themes in literature.
B. Makes connections between novel's themes and personal view of contemporary society.
C. The writer calls this piece a critical analysis. Instead, the writer uses the literary experience to evaluate the world around her, drawing connections between her observations and the events and point of view in the book. In a strict sense, we get very little analysis of the book itself.

Critical Analysis   Mrs. Dalloway

A. "The world has raised its whip, where will it descend?...nobody knows." In fact, the possibility it will fall our way is greater than ever imaginable. It is true, human nature is out to get us...everyone is at the mercy of the world.

B. Human beings worry only about themselves. The fact is, the world puts people down and keeps them there. Society searches for the feeble and frail to satisfy its hunger for power, allowing nothing to get in its way. People ask for help and they will only be deserted. Control is the ultimate desire and to obtain it is the greatest goal. The reality is, our lives are being manipulated to suit society's needs. As human beings we need to face reality and deal with the negative occurrences head on. Even though things are difficult, we must be positive and live life to the fullest, not allowing society to dictate our existence.

C. Human beings worry only about themselves..."For the truth is that human beings have neither kindness, nor faith, nor charity beyond what serves to increase their pleasures of the moment."

D. Links thematic quote from novel to description of specific characters and then to the real-world business practices of used-car salespeople.
E. Unified reflection on materialism and used cars.

D. There was Brewer at the office, with his waxed moustache, coral tiepin, white slip, and pleasurable emotions-all cold and clamminess within; or Amelia, handing round cups of tea punctually at five-a leering, sneering obscene little harpy; and the Toms and Berties in their starched shirt fronts oozing thick drops of vice.

E. With the fast paced environment we live in, vehicles have become an essential part of daily living. It is obvious car salesmen have only one mission: to sell as many cars as they possibly can...regardless of the condition of the car. They will try to deceive us by making us feel confident about a vehicle. An automobile's fine appearance and glamorous shine will often sweep buyers off their feet, and they are content to ignore the facts. If the odometer only reads 15,000 miles, we assume, Wow! What a bargain. When in fact, the odometer has been tampered with and what we're buying is "a lemon". Sure, fooling around with these cards in such a manner is a federal offense, but the dealers are so greedy, they are willing to put their "business" on the line...all for money. It doesn't matter that they are swindling innocent people out of their hard earned money. They love to boast about their "earnings" and how hard they worked to get it. When buying a car, we can never investigate the history of that car enough...who knows what we'll find?!!!!

No matter what, society will always search for the feeble and frail to satisfy its hunger for power. They will use any means to get what they want...deception being a great one. "They hunt in packs. Their packs scour the desert and vanish screaming into the wilderness." People search high and low for anyone and anything to feed on...almost as if they are a pack of hungry lions, circling around a wounded wildebeest. They take from people who can't or won't stick up for themselves. A little bit of power here and a bit there...it all adds up. It matters not about your gender, race or daily preferences...we will be hunted down, and pay the price for simply being in the wrong place at the wrong time. There they wait...

"...feasting on the wills of the weakly, loving to impress, to impose, adoring their own features stamped on the face of the populace."

Society searches for suckers who will fall for anything...luring them closer and closer into its trap until the precise moment when the masses can pounce and suffocate victims. . . . .

The desire for control is overpowering. Corruption…the power to run the world in any fashion. Corruption is lying to the underdogs, manipulating them into believing what they know is wrong and what society wants is for the best. Society is trying to create its own utopia…a world where everything is perfect in the eyes of the masses. "Human nature forces us to be something we aren't." It plays with our minds and forces us to become

F. what they want us to be and not what we truly are. Innocent people are placed into uncomfortable positions…controlled by an opposing force they only want to hide from. "Are we all not prisoners," of this mind-trap? We must break free from these chains that bind us to the confinement of the walls…we must escape.

"The soul must brave itself to endure." If only Septimus

G. wouldn't have given in, he'd have gone so far. The world devoured him in a single bite…it was all over for him. Septimus chose to end his life, thereby ending the pain and suffering he was going through. There were better ways to solve his problems then by resorting to suicide. There are always positive solutions to any situation…searching for them takes time, but time will pay off in the long run. Human nature can be overcome. We can learn to stand once we have fallen and be strong once again.

Human nature is out to get us, but rest assured…there is an

H. escape from it all. This escape is called solitude. It is possible to achieve this if we only have faith in ourselves and believe that with patience, anything is possible. Though the whip may fall, as long as we are strong…it will never fall our way.

F. Begins to suggest possible solutions for problems identified earlier.
G. Concludes each paragraph with a positive suggestion.
H. Concluding paragraph refers back to opening quotation.

Connections to Standards

Natalie demonstrates substantial achievement in:

● reading literature to build an understanding of the many dimensions of human experience (2);

● applying knowledge of media techniques, figurative language, and genre to critique a literary text (6).

T a s k

Reading journals often show the reader/writer questioning and talking back and forth to self about the ideas in the book. Sometimes the journal is simply a stream of consciousness–an interior monologue of impressions that arise during reading.

Commentary

Excerpt from reading journal shows how Natalie used the idea of "feasting on the wills of the weakly" as a springboard for exploring images of wild animals hunting.

> * "...Feasting on the wills of the weakly
> It reminds me of a vaccuum that goes around sucking up everything within it's reach that isn't securely attached to a base
> People search high and low for anyone and everyone to feed on ... almost as if they are a pack of hungry lions, circling around a wounded antelope wildabeast
> They took from anyone that can't or won't stick-up for themselves ... thereby becoming the culprit of a mischievous act. It matters not about your gender, race or daily preferences ... you will be hunted down, and pay for simply being in the wrong place at the wrong time.

Commentary

Excerpt from reading journal shows Natalie identified opening quote as "hook." The notes indicate she was considering using "Are we not all prisoners?" as conclusion, but evidently changed her mind and returned to opening quote instead.

Connections to Standards

Natalie demonstrates substantial achievement in:

• applying a wide range of strategies to comprehend, interpret, evaluate, and appreciate a literary text (3).

> *Prejudice Jews Blacks*
> * "Feasting on the wills of the weakly." p.135 for the truth is that human being have niether kindness, nor faith, nor charity beyond what serves to increase their pleasures of the moment.
> * They hunt in packs, their packs scour the desert and vanish screaming into the wilderness. They desert the fallen / He swooped : devoured : shut people up.
> *Circumstancial evidence*
> p.139 * If you make one mistake their once you stumb human nature is upon you.
> * "Human nature is remorseless"
> * "Human nature forces you to be something you aren't"
> * "are we all not prisoners?" ← END
> HOOK ← The world has raised its whip: where will it descend, nobody knows
> * "He would argue with her, about killing themselves because he knew how wicked people were; he could see them making up lies. He knew all their thoughts, he knew the meaning of the world."

Task

On the portfolio entry slip, Natalie writes that this piece began in ninth grade as a response to reading *Lord of the Flies*. In tenth grade, she says, "I began editing and reworking the piece to enter it in the <u>USA Today</u> short story contest." Not included here are the numerous and extensively revised drafts that accompanied this piece in Natalie's whole portfolio as evidence of her use of writing processes and strategies. About the development of the piece, Natalie writes, "The final copy . . . is very unlike the first draft. It has undergone severe changes which I feel are for the better. It leaves the reader on the edge and leaves them room to wonder about the ending. This paper was written for the soul [*sic*] purpose of being creative . . . nothing more."

**Writing in a
Literary Genre: Short Story**

High

Rubric / Commentary

A. The three opening words reinforce ominous tone of title.
B. Interior monologue introduces and reveals the character of the narrator.
C. In the sequence, the trials (gum, revealed crush, braid) are presented as equal horrors. The narrator's grip on the world is in doubt at this point.

Tragedy in the Water

A.   Cold…Sleep…Water…

Friends I've had in my life…makes me wonder why I ever bothered. I tried so hard to please everyone. All I ever wanted was to be accepted…to be cool. All that was ever given to me in return was a snide look or a taunting laugh. Hey Pat, thanks for the time you stuck gum on my seat in the middle of English class
B. and when I got up to go sharpen my pencil, the whole class noticed and laughed at me for the rest of the day. Thanks Jane, for the time when you promised you wouldn't tell John I had an enormous crush on him and then you broadcasted it to the entire school over the PA system during morning announcements. Oh, and Marie, I really enjoyed it when you cut off my braid in the locker room and I didn't notice it was gone until Mrs. Pytlak asked me why I cut my beautiful hair, and after school I found my braid hanging from the flag pole. So much humiliation and I
C. took it day after day…if only the kids would've given me half a chance, I know I could've proved them wrong. Just once, I'd like to do something so brave so I'd certainly be worthy of their praise. What I wouldn't give to have one last chance to prove myself capable and maybe even a hero…things weren't looking very bright at the moment.

I was fighting for all I was worth. The rocks beneath me were being kicked around so much I swear they were alive. For a split second, the thought of letting go of my creatively crafted

Paper continued on page 64

D. Interweaves interior monologue with story events.

E. Many concrete details contribute to setting.

F. Precise language helps keep the plot moving.

G. Transition from dusk to dawn managed skillfully.

H. "Fiddling" seems an off-the-mark choice. "Struggling" seems more consistent. But maybe inconsistency is what the writer wants to convey.

D. fishing pole ran through my mind. I'd expertly crafted my pole with a long, bamboo rod. I was proud of my work and I just couldn't bear the thought of throwing it all away. I struggled a bit longer, my hopes growing dimmer every second. Suddenly, the rock beneath me gave way. It activated the rock beside it and the next thing I knew, words of excruciating pain were echoing

E. from my mouth. A large boulder had fallen onto my left foot, pinning me to the ocean floor. Now what am I supposed to do? Grabbing my knife from my pocket, I sliced the line on my pole and released the fish. My grasp on the bamboo rod tightened. How could I have been so stupid? Now I'm trapped in the water and there's nowhere to run.

Surviving the worst night of my life gave me new hope. I

F. had been submerged under the water for almost twelve hours and the water level would soon be receding. Maybe my friends are worried about me? Oh, I wish I could go back and reassure them I'm okay. I'm sure they'll be excited to hear about my misadventure and how I bravely won the battle against the ocean…or then again, maybe not.

The sunrise was beautiful to watch. It meant I had endured

G. the awful night. Although the sunrise seemed blurry, it wasn't as blurry as the moon had been last night. Reaching my free hand straight up I was amazed to discover my hand broke the surface. All right! The tide's going out. Maybe there is hope after all.

Half an hour later my nose broke the surface. It won't be long now, I thought…

When the tide had gone out fully, I allowed my body to relax. The only problem remaining was my trapped foot still cap…hoping it wasn't waterlogged. The next thing I found myself doing was attempting to pry the rock off my foot with my bamboo stick. At first it was to no avail, but determination kept me going. I contemplated the reactions of my friends when they found my drowned corpse. They'll probably just brush my death aside like I never existed. I have to prove myself worthy of their praise. I just have to. Sheer stubbornness kept me going. I

H. continued fiddling around the rock, approaching it at as many angles as were possible. The rock was at a slant and when I wedged my stick underneath, it rolled just enough for my foot to slide free. The toes of my foot pointed in all directions and my foot throbbed out of control. I swam slowly to the edge of the sand and fell into a deep sleep. A bizarre dream invaded my mind. I was submerged under the water and was drowning. Time and time again screams poured from my mouth, but my screams were futile. I woke up screaming…my stick clenched in my fist. Uhh, what a horrible nightmare. Looking around I found it hadn't been a nightmare…it was for real. The sight of my badly bruised foot made my worst nightmares a reality and I just wanted to get as far from the water as possible…

I heard the gang was down at the arcade so I figured I'd mozey on down and share my adventure with them. They have to accept me now…they just have to. Upon reaching the arcade, I saw everyone huddled in a circle, chatting amongst themselves. Casually, I sauntered over and joined the group. A silence fell over the circle and I attempted to break the uneasiness; I tried to recount the experience I'd had the week before. Everyone began talking at once, trying to drown me out…making me feel unwelcome and unwanted. No one would even give me the chance to tell how brave I'd been. As I was pushed from the circle, an overwhelming fear consumed my body, seizing my breath and causing me to feel light-headed. In the back of my mind all I could hear were the taunting jeers and mocking laughter of everyone.

A suffocating darkness all around…cold…sleep…water…

I. Description of escape detailed and believable.

J. Returns to acceptance theme.

K. The ending repeats the opening line, showing the writer's awareness of form.

L. Concludes on note of uncertainty—did the narrator actually drown or not?

Connections to Standards

Natalie demonstrates substantial achievement in:

- using writing to communicate effectively with a particular audience for a specific purpose (5);

- applying knowledge of language structure, language conventions, figurative language, and genre to create a literary text (6);

- using writing to accomplish her own purposes (12).

T a s k

Students were asked to include in their portfolios examples of multiple drafts of one or more selections. The purpose of this assignment is to track how well students use the editing and drafting process to develop a work. Two drafts are presented here.

C o m m e n t a r y

First page of original story draft. "I thought of all the times the kids in my school had been mean to me" has been expanded with specific instances into the first paragraph of the final story. Connections to *Lord of the Flies* are obvious in first draft, but have all but disappeared from final draft.

Tragedy in the Water

Draft I

As I beat my way through the tangled underbrush, I thought of all the times the kids in my school had been mean to me. It hadn't always been intentional, but it still hurt. I would show them now. Maybe being a hero and keeping my friends and myself alive on this island would prove to them

Something very important:

~~that~~ just because you aren't one of the cool kids, doesn't mean ~~that~~ you are a nobody.

My mission today was to get something for supper. ~~So~~

until now,

we'd

far all ~~we had~~ been living on were coconuts and bananas. All of the other kids, ~~said~~ ~~~~, were too lazy to go find something decent to eat, *so I decided to show them up.*

I was able to

Working diligently all morning, ~~I~~ created a state of

Big deal

the art fishing pole. ~~So what~~ if it wasn't ~~~~ original. ~~but~~

Hopefully it would help to keep us alive. ~~~~ *construct~~ing~~*

it with a long, sturdy piece of bamboo, ~~I~~ I expertly secured a piece of twine for the fishing line. To serve as

was attached.

hook, ~~~~ a small safety pin. Up to the present time, I

could be used

hadn't ~~~~ decided what ~~~~ ~~~~ for ~~the~~ bait, but ~~I~~ decided

it was

to climb that hill when ~~I~~ reached ~~it.~~

my

I had been walking for about three hours when ~~I~~ ~~heard~~

gave a ferocious

my stomach growl...Quite loudly I might add. "Boy, am I glad

are around They'd let me

that none of the other kids ~~heard that.~~ ~~I would~~ never ~~hear the~~

live it down

~~end of it.~~ I'll show them...just wait.

seeing

~~~~ a clearing up ahead, so I quickened my pace. ~~What~~

The view through the clearing

~~saw then~~ was spectacular. The ocean was spread out in

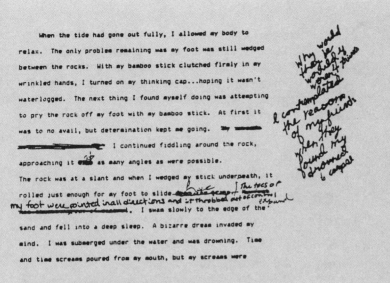

When the tide had gone out fully, I allowed my body to
relax. The only problem remaining was my foot was still wedged
between the rocks. With my bamboo stick clutched firmly in my
wrinkled hands, I turned on my thinking cap...hoping it wasn't
waterlogged. The next thing I found myself doing was attempting
to pry the rock off my foot with my bamboo stick. At first it
was to no avail, but determination kept me going.

I continued fiddling around the rock,
approaching it at as many angles as were possible.
The rock was at a slant and when I wedged my stick underneath, it
rolled just enough for my foot to slide. I swam slowly to the edge of the
sand and fell into a deep sleep. A bizarre dream invaded my
mind. I was submerged under the water and was drowning. Time
and time screams poured from my mouth, but my screams were

futile. I woke up screaming, my stick clenched in my fist. Uhh,
what a horrible nightmare. Looking around I found it hadn't been
a nightmare...it was for real.
With my beloved
bamboo stick, I swatted the nearest coconut to the ground and
penetrated the skin with my knife. My knife was rusted
quite badly, but I managed to cut the coconut open. The
milk soothed my dry throat.

I was ready to head back to the others when I realized
nothing had been collected for supper. I'd better dig some clams
or nothing will change...I won't be a hero. Hurriedly, I dug
three dozen clams with my bamboo stick because the tide was
coming in. They were gathered and placed in my tattered shirt.
Looking at the sun, I assumed it was four o'clock. I'm really
going to have to hurry if I want to get back before dusk, the
tee-pee is a good two hours from here.

It was a long journey, but soon I could see the smoke
from our fire wafting up towards the sky. Traveling had been
difficult with my shattered ankle. Almost home, I thought. The
last few steps to the clearing I took long and slow. Upon
reaching the clearing, the guys spotted me. One of them fainted.
I shouted, Hey guys, look what I've got. Oh, and you'll never
believe what happened.

With that, I raised my bamboo stick high above my head
for victory and limped to my friends.

Commentary

(Last page of later story draft). Note
how Natalie has responded to
teacher's marginal comments.
The original conclusion is quite
different from the conclusion of
the final draft. The final version
is much darker in tone and returns to the theme of acceptance
which appears in the beginning
of the story.

Connections to Standards

Natalie demonstrates substantial
achievement in:

● employing a wide range of
strategies as she writes and using
different writing process elements
appropriately (5).

Task

Natalie's teacher certified that Natalie had read the works she listed below. Her teacher wrote that Natalie "has become an avid reader and she yearns for good literature....She connects themes from different texts and she can discuss creative comparisons and contrasts verbally and in writing.... This portfolio portrays a year of hard work."

Rubric

The requirements for breadth in reading were
- at least twenty-five books (or equivalent);
- a balance of literature and non-literary works;
- at least three different genres or modes;
- at least five different authors;
- at least four books by the same author, in the same genre, or about one topic.

Les Livres

"Every time I open a book, I risk my life...Every work of imagination offers another view of life, an invitation to spend a few days inside someone else's emotions."

-Anatole Broyard

The list below represents the books I have read this past year...in our English curriculum and outside of class during my free time.

Cowboys Don't Cry, Marilyn Halvorson-A Young boy struggles to live a normal life with his father.

The Face on the Milk Carton, Caroline B. Cooney-Janie discovers the truth of the face on the milk carton...now she must live with the information she's uncovered.

Whatever Happened to Janie?, Caroline B. Cooney-Janie must choose between the family she truly loves, or the family she can't seem to get along with.

A Solitary Blue, Cynthia Voigt-A familiar story dealing with the pain of living life after your parents have gotten divorced.

The Gift, Peter Dickinson-Davey has the gift of seeing into other people's minds, but people don't always think good thoughts...not even the people you love.

The Moonstone, Wilkie Collins-When the curse finds you...you've found the Moonstone.

The Young Pitcher, Zane Grey-It's proof that hard work and sheer stubbornness will help you achieve any goal...no matter its size or shape.

Maine Ghosts and Legends, Thomas A. Verde-Don't turn around...the kiss of death may be creeping up behind you.

The Beans of Egypt, ME., Caroline Chute-The story of and "interesting" family living in the Maine woods.

The House of Mirth, Edith Wharton-A frail woman's struggle to keep pace with the high society life of New York City.

Taking Care of Terrific, Lois Lowry-The touching story of a young boy and his babysitter's caring relationship for the homeless of their town.

The Moon is Broken, Eleanor Craig-A dramatic, true story of a young woman's desperate fight against drugs and AIDS.

<u>Fair Game</u>, Erika Tamar-What seemed to be an innocent day after school, turned out to be the worst mistake the boys would ever make.

<u>Ordinary People</u>, Judith Guest-A story of a death…an attempted suicide and a family who must cope with the problems they have.

<u>Ghost Girl</u>, Torey Hayden-The shocking, true story of a traumatized young child's battle to emerge from her "shell".

<u>The Scarlet Letter</u>, Nathaniel Hawthorne-Hester was condemned for a sin which time would never erase…it had been etched into her heart forever.

<u>A Day No Pigs Would Die</u>, Robert Newton Peck-The hard lessons you learn in life will forever be with you…

<u>Mrs. Dalloway</u>, Virginia Woolf-The desire to regain childhood is often over-powering and Clarissa would ignore the realities of life to obtain it.

<u>Dying for Chocolate</u>, Diane Mott Davidson-A deceitful caterer's murder mystery that holds you in suspense until the last page.

<u>Brave New World</u>, Aldous Huxley-It's a whole new world where everything is being controlled to suit society's needs.

<u>The Giver</u>, Lois Lowry-Everyone is assigned roles in the community. Everything seemed so perfect…then Jonas began thinking…

<u>Fahrenheit 451</u>, Ray Bradbury-Books must have significance if the old lady was willing to die for them. Montag was determined to discover the truth…the only thing still in his way…Fahrenheit 451.

<u>Much Ado About Nothing</u>, William Shakespeare-A hilarious comedy with romance and deception galore.

<u>Hamlet</u>, William Shakespeare-Young Hamlet must avenge his father's death, but is murder the best way to solve the problem?

<u>Loves Music, Loves to Dance</u>, Mary Higgins Clark-The murderer is out there, waiting for the music to start…calling for him to kill again.

<u>All Around the Town</u>, Mary Higgins Clark-How may times will she have to relive that awful kidnapping over in her head? It may not be for much longer because her multiple personalities are slowly taking over.

<u>While My Pretty One Sleeps</u>, Mary Higgins Clark-That rapping on the window is not the wind…he's come for revenge…will you be ready?

<u>A Stranger is Watching</u>, Mary Higgins Clark-He'd abducted her because she'd ruined his life, now he was going to ruin hers. It was only a matter of time before the bomb went off and ended her life.

<u>The Runner</u>, Cynthia Voigt-Bullet ran because it made him feel good. He did it for himself and for nobody else. He would learn the hard way that someday, life will catch up with you.

<u>The Jungle</u>, Upton Sinclair-The repulsive and brutish story of the unsanitary conditions of the Chicago stockyards.

Commentary

Introductory quote suggests how Natalie views reading.

Succinct comments reflect engagement with reading.

List of thirty books (and book-length works) represent good balance between classic and contemporary texts.

Shows in-depth reading in one author (Mary Higgins Clark) and genre (e.g., mystery, science fiction).

List could have included informational texts read for research project on women in baseball.

Connections to Standards

Natalie demonstrates substantial achievement in:

• reading a wide range of classic and contemporary works (1);

• reading a wide range of literature from many periods in many genres (2).

Research Project

Task

Throughout the year, students in Natalie's class kept autobiographical journals which included, among other topics, reflections on childhood memories. Students also read literature dealing with censorship of thought and the death of imagination (e.g., *The Giver*, *Fahrenheit 451*, "Harrison Bergeron," "The Veldt"). This research project explored the following questions: Does TV kill kids' imagination? Should the public be concerned about television programming? Does your autobiographical journal show lack of childhood imagination? Is imagination important for intellectual growth? In order to answer these questions, Natalie interviewed children and adults about their television viewing habits, analyzed children's television programming, reviewed her autobiographical journal for evidence, and wrote a final reflection summing up her findings. Six excerpts of Natalie's project are presented here: a paper, interview notes, interview report, cartoon notes, cartoon analysis, and an autobiography. This project shows one of the great strengths of the portfolio as an assessment device. Here we have six different pieces, all connected by one project, each one showing evidence of different dimensions of the standards.

EXCERPT 1: PAPER

Rubric / Commentary

In this research project, the last step is an argument based on the research. Natalie argues for ratings on T.V. shows.

A. Opens with strong personal statement.

B. Informal tone appropriate to purpose.

C. Presents sound reasons for advocating censorship and shows awareness that many readers may disagree.

Final Conclusions

A. Television definitely does kill kids imagination. I personally feel kids aren't as imaginative today as they were many years ago. With the invention of television, more and more kids are turning into couch potatoes, frying their brain on the junk shows now playing. Instead of reading, writing or going outside to play, they now sit inside all day and do absolutely nothing but let their eyes get tired. Kids are learning violence from TV and they are using it in their everyday lives…not **B.** even realizing what they are doing is wrong. Hey, if the TV superheroes can do it and it is good, then why can't I? I have a feeling that is often times the attitude many kids have.

At this date in time, I feel it necessary that something be done about the programs that are played on the television. **C.** Ratings have been put on movies so young kids only watch movies which are appropriate for their age level. The same should be true for the television programs they also watch. Something must be done to prevent the further downfall of kids imagination. A lot of people may disagree with me on the censorship deal. They don't feel these programs are having bad effects on childrens lives. All I need to say to them is, can you please explain where a five year old gets the idea to go out and shoot someone? I don't think they thought it up themselves.

As far as my personal Autobiographical Journals are concerned, they don't show lack of imagination. I have been very fortunate to have such wonderful parents who care very much about me and they didn't raise me watching violence on television. I did watch a lot of TV from time to time, but it was mostly all educational and funny. When I was young, I used to spend as much time outside playing as I did watching television. I am very lucky to have two younger brothers, and together, we made up some great games and always had a blast.

D.

Without imagination, I would have a very hard time growing intellectually. Throughout grade school, I met new and bigger challenges that helped me broaden my imagination and I used it all the time. Through these accomplishments, I have grown so much it is unbelievable. It just goes to show you how important imagination really is and why young kids need to have the opportunities I've had to grow and work with their imaginations to become mature individuals. Imagination is not a one time deal. You use it everyday of your entire life and it will never go away. It's very important that you have a big imagination than not having one at all…it's just something that helps make you a great person.

E.

D. Incorporates material from auto-biographical journal.
E. A rather weak conclusion in which Natalie tries to link personal experience to some broader statements about the value of imagination.

Connections to Standards

Natalie demonstrates substantial achievement in:

● conducting research on an issue of interest; gathering, analyzing, and synthesizing data from a variety of sources; and communicating her discoveries in a way that suits her purpose and audience (7).

Commentary

Natalie has prepared a list of interview questions on her topic and has noted the responses from the first interview.

Connections to Standards

Natalie demonstrates substantial achievement in:

● gathering data from a variety of sources (7).

TELEVISION / IMAGINATION PROJECT
8 years old
Child Interview

1) What is your favorite thing to do?

ride your bike outside
on nice summer day
goes for rides to the park

2) How much TV do you watch in a day? What shows?

only a little.
alegria's window
little bits
cartoons
mostly all she watches are cartoon-type shows
or movies like Dennis the Menace.

3) How much TV do you watch on Saturdays? What shows?

alot
Beethoven
Aladdin
Garfield.
Little Mermaid
Then goes shopping with her mother
doesn't watch Teenage mutant Ninja Turtles

4) Why do you like the shows you watch?

funny and entertaining
likes animals

5) Do you like to read? Why or why not?

yes. books are interesting
minnie mouse
Tom Sawyer
Borenstein Bears

Child Interview…TV Project

After interviewing my eight year old cousin, I learned that she doesn't watch a lot of television. Her mother monitors what she watches. The shows that she does watch aren't violent, like the cartoon Skeleton Warriors. The shows and cartoons which she watches on Saturday and during the week are more or less educational. She learns about animals and nature in these shows and finds them very interesting. They teach her new things and from this she makes up games or even draws pictures of her favorite cartoons, like Minnie Mouse. The effects of TV on her seem to be a positive one to me. The main reason I believe this is so is because she doesn't spend all of her time sitting in front of the boob tube. After school hours are spent outside, riding her bike or playing games with her mother or younger sister. One game she told me about which she invented is called "Swing Tag." Someone lies on their belly on a swing. People walk by and the person on the swing tries to tag them. She also likes to make up stories about horses and then illustrate them with drawings she makes of horses. Books are a big part of her life and she spends most of her time reading. School is extremely enjoyable for her and her favorite part of the day is when they form reading groups and read to each other out loud.

She told me that when she grows up she would like to become a veterinarian and take care of animals, because they mean a lot to her and she loves to be around them. Through reading, watching educational shows and being inventive in her writing and drawing, she is building a strong imagination and this is a great base for her future. She is going to be a great person to hang around with and talk to. I believe imagination makes a person what they are and what they will become. In my opinion, creative people make the best workers. My cousin is getting all of the exposure she needs to be a truly creative person and she will be successful.

Commentary

Natalie's formal account of interview with a child. From the very sketchy notes shown, she has constructed a highly readable text.

Here, Natalie evaluates the information obtained from the interview.

Connections to Standards

Natalie demonstrates substantial achievement in:

• synthesizing data from a variety of sources (7).

Commentary

An interview plan is one form of data collection. An observation plan is another form. Shown here is Natalie's data collection form for an observation of the cartoon "The Little Mermaid." This observation provided data for the analysis shown on page 75.

Connections to Standards

Natalie demonstrates substantial achievement in:

• gathering data from a variety of sources (7).

CARTOON ANALYSIS SHEET

Name of Cartoon: The Little Mermaid
Date: February 4, 1995
Time: 8:00 am
Day: Saturday

1) Number of violent/inappropriate acts noted in the show. Please give explanations of at least 5 of these acts.

little evil manta is torturing baby catfish
throws paint at the mermaids
destroys Flounders sculpture
Sebastian gets electrocuted by Evil manta
Big Evil manta destroys art gallery
lock ariel in a cave
Brain sponge bit Big Evil
Dropped rock on brain sponge
Big evil has a brain sponge to suck out ariel's imagination

(Nome's imagination would overide take on away)

Jar of screams
Evil Eye - things to destroy

Big Evil manta sings lull-a-bye to little evil. have terrifying dreams, be wicked, calls him rotten have a real bad night

2) In your opinion, what is the plot of the cartoon?
while ariel is searching for inspiration for her art sculpture, she meets little Evil and from then on she tries her best to make him good and prevent him from becoming evil like his father. Big evil learns of ariel's plan and he tries to get rid of her imagination by having his brain sponge suck it out. Little Evil does good and saves her life. Big evil realizes little evil feels better doing good and he honors his opinions.

3) Why do you think this cartoon appeals/does not appeal to kids? Explain. I think it appeals more to the younger kids 2-6 years. It's a very peaceful cartoon in contrast to Skeleton warriers which is action packed. The older kids - 6-10 probably feel it's more of a baby show and doesn't have enough action in it for them. The creatures on the show are young and imaginitive like the young kids and they like that. Monkey see... monkey do! The older kids want to grow up and they think it's a waste of time to watch a baby show.

Cartoon Analysis…TV Project

Bam, smash, crash is mostly all I heard throughout the cartoon show Skeleton Warriors. It's the usual good vs. bad type cartoon where good must keep the evil from becoming the dominant force. Kids who watch this show are getting the impression that these violent acts are okay because in order for the good to defeat the bad sometimes, they have to do bad things and this makes them no better than the evil ones. They fight fire with fire and the kids see and they apply it to their everyday lives. If you get punched in the face, they think it's okay to punch back and get even. They don't stop to think who or what they are hurting, they just act.

What's really bad is that innocent cartoons even contain violence, they always have. Take for instance, The Little Mermaid, which I watched and analyzed. Even in this cartoon I found many acts of violence which don't seem like they would have any effect on the children, and if you think about it, these acts are so nonchalant you don't notice them at all. Sooner or later the kids will just incorporate such acts into their lifestyles and they will become habitual.

Even though there is violence on TV, the message of the show can be a very positive one. The Little Mermaid cartoon I happened to see is a perfect example. In this cartoon, kids learn how important it is to have an imagination and to never be afraid to use it. Also, that it is okay to be good and go against the crowd and not be drug down by peer pressure…your good ways won't go unnoticed. They learn that sometimes you have to make a personal decision and do what feels right.

Kids are like vacuums and they will suck up any and all trash which is tossed in front of them. This includes the "garbage" shown on television or games at the arcade, or entertainment systems like Nintendo or Sega Genesis. Television is getting way out of hand and something needs to be done. I feel censoring shows would be a good idea, maybe not a popular one, but an important one for our future generations.

Commentary

Natalie completed an analysis of several T.V. shows in her research project. One of these was her analysis of "The Little Mermaid," shown here. This analysis evaluates the positive and negative impact of T.V.

Connections to Standards

Natalie demonstrates substantial achievement in:

• synthesizing data from a variety of sources (7).

Commentary

Research projects often require students to connect their personal experience to the research topic. Sometimes these personal connections are part of the research log or journal in which students log their various research steps and their personal responses. In the selection here, Natalie writes a more formal autobiographical account of her experiences with T.V. and its impact on her reading.

Connections to Standards

Natalie demonstrates substantial achievement in:

• gathering, evaluating, and synthesizing data from a variety of sources (in this case, reflection on personal experience) and communicating her discoveries in ways that suit her purpose and audience (7).

I am the luckiest person in the world to have parents like mine. They are so much fun. When I was five years old, Mom took us to Memere and Pepere's house for a picnic. She showed us her old treehouse. We all climbed up in it and had our special lunch which Mom had packed in our new lunchboxes. She told us a story about the time when she went for a walk in the woods with her brothers and they had a picnic similar to ours. They got scared by a loud crash which they all thought was a bear, so they high tailed it for home.

One of the first games I learned to play outside was Hide and Go Seek. All of the neighborhood kids would come over to my house and we would pick someone to be it. We also played Kick the Can, which is my all-time favorite game.

On Saturdays I got up early and drug Mom out of bed. We always watched cartoons together. Sometimes I would pick and sometimes Mom would pick. After we watched a little bit of TV, I would put my play clothes on and go out and play in the sandbox with by brother. We loved to play with matchbox cars and Tonka trucks. We would create tunnels and make roads to travel on. Sometimes we would pretend there was an earthquake and the roads would all get destroyed.

On rainy days, Mom made us hot chocolate and we listened to her read a book. My favorite one was <u>Snow Lion</u>.

I'm glad my childhood was so much fun. When I look around today, I feel really sorry for all the kids who weren't as fortunate as I was to have opportunities to do such great stuff. All they did all day was watch TV and as far as I'm concerned, TV rots your brain and too much of it is bad for your health. Mom has enough books to read to last me a lifetime. She loves to read more than I do. I only hope someday I am as great of a person as she is.

Summary Commentary of Natalie's Portfolio

Natalie's portfolio shows that she has attained a substantial level of achievement in the English language arts. The artifacts presented here suggest that Natalie has excellent encoding skills. In writing, her work exhibits virtual mastery of many language structures and of most conventions, such as spelling, usage, and punctuation. While some errors are noticeable (e.g., frequent neglect of apostrophe), they are not distracting. From a cognitive perspective, the quantity and quality of the reading evidence (e.g., background reading for baseball paper, analysis of Virginia Woolf novel *Mrs. Dalloway,* reading list) suggest that Natalie is a fluent reader who comprehends a range of challenging ideas and a range of literary and informational texts. One judge who scored Natalie's portfolio commented

> 'Critical Analysis' piece in particular shows a variety of responses to the material, including personal, literal, and critical. Throughout the portfolio, the evaluative stance is evidenced through appropriate and consistent use of literary sources.

The evidence in Natalie's portfolio suggests that she is skilled at processing information and using a variety of strategies to understand and to represent ideas. Her range of cognitive skills is impressive. She sketches, outlines, brainstorms, drafts, and re-drafts. Her letter of introduction and the excerpts from entry slips also show that Natalie is aware of her reading and writing processes, that she can set and achieve specific goals, and that she can articulate both strengths and weaknesses. At the sentence level, Natalie uses coordination and subordination skillfully and effectively varies sentence structure and length. In the "TV Programming Project," Natalie demonstrates that she can conduct research using primary sources. Natalie's portfolio contains several examples of her rhetorical ability to translate information into forms appropriate for various audiences. For example, "Women in Baseball," "To Achieve or not to Achieve," and the analysis of *Mrs. Dalloway* have very different patterns of organization, but each is appropriate for audience and purpose. Her range of audiences includes readers of the high school newspaper ("To Achieve or Not to Achieve"), *USA Today* readers ("Tragedy in the Water"), classmates ("Women in Baseball"), teacher, readers of the portfolio, and self ("*Mrs. Dalloway:* A Critical Analysis," dialectical journals). The editorial, the persuasive essay, and the television research project are good examples of Natalie's attention to the needs of her audience.

Natalie writes in a variety of forms, including reflective essay, response to literature, persuasive essay, short story, and newspaper article. Natalie also reads and responds to a broad range of materials, as her reading list suggests. One judge who scored Natalie's portfolio commented

> shows a wide range of reading types, various uses and responses to information read . . . accepts reading challenges and explores and makes meaning within, between, and beyond text.

Natalie's portfolio entries show that she is conversant with key concepts in English. For example, the short story "Tragedy in the Water" demonstrates that Natalie understands and can control such elements as point of view, plot, setting, and theme. Her analysis of *Mrs. Dalloway* shows that she applies concepts such as theme and symbolism to a close reading of the text. The portfolio provides numerous examples that Natalie deals skillfully and insightfully with cultural ideas, such as the tensions between self-interest and the well-being of society (*Mrs. Dalloway*), between the need for self-reliance and the need to belong ("Tragedy in the Water"), between the role of imagination and the role of experience ("TV Programming Project"). In fact, the whole portfolio may be seen as developing in one way or another the theme stated on its title page: "This above all; to thine own self be true."

Overall, Natalie's portfolio demonstrates that she has a high level of conceptual knowledge (knowing that) which enables her to read and write fluently, performance knowledge (knowing how) which enables her to read a broad range of texts and write in a variety of genres, and background knowledge (knowing about) which enables her to perform well at almost every task she has undertaken for this portfolio. While a reader of Natalie's portfolio can easily perceive ways in which Natalie might improve her reading and writing even more (e.g., read more nonfiction texts, eliminate usage and spelling errors in final pieces, set more specific literacy goals), Natalie's work is unquestionably in the high range of performance.

Portfolios

Natalie

Loretta

Terry

Loretta compiled this portfolio at the end of her tenth-grade year, attempting to represent the work she completed over the course of the school year. We have selected only a few pieces for inclusion here. Some of the pieces are excerpts only. You may want to review some of the portfolio requirements listed on page 45.

Task

Many portfolios require that students write a reflective essay reviewing strengths and weaknesses in the work in the portfolio. The student is, at the same time, preparing readers of the portfolio for what is to follow.

Reflective Essay
(Letter)

Middle

Letter of Introduction

This 1994-1995 school year,   High School took on the challenge of the New Standards Portfolio Project.

A. In English IV-   this year I accomplished a lot. I learned how to write a character analysis, basically by breaking the story into parts and analyzing it completely. I also learned how to construct essays in different writing styles. My biggest accomplishment, I feel, was the correct way to engineer a research paper.

B. As the year went by, I found how my writing techniques advanced and how I became a better writer. I still have my weakness in gathering information and putting it together, but it's becoming easier.

C. This portfolio contains my best work throughout the year. Each piece has helped prepare me for the future I have in college.

Rubric / Commentary

A. States specific accomplishments in writing in various genres.
B. General reference to improved writing techniques.
C. Shows understanding of purpose of this portfolio.

Task

The entry slip for this piece acknowledges that it is a draft for a "final speech." Loretta added that she delivered the speech in a local contest and "received first place" for it.

Rubric / Commentary

A. Engages reader (listener) interest by establishing a common bond—a shared hometown. Demonstrates familiarity with media techniques used to promote towns and cities.

B. Shows awareness of community issues. Appeals to audience concerns—lost jobs and population depletion.

C. Enhances authority by naming other possible topics.

D. Presents well-organized evidence to support claim that a county hospital is needed.

A. Z_____. . . .the place where the sun spends the winter. . . .home of beautiful Falcon Lake and a proud community where history and culture live in the heart of its people. Though a small town, it is where most of us have grown up and where our memories of childhood will always dwell. This is our home.

B. Z_____ is rapidly expanding and growing in population. Our county's prosperitiy is due to several factos, two of which are the growing number of winter T ____s making Z_____ their permanent residences, and the abundance of oil and gas reserves. When these resources are exhausted our tax-base will be diminished and along with it, economic growth and expansion will be limited. This would result in decreased population, because people, especially the younger generation, would be forced to leave Z_____ in search of jobs.

C. So in answering the proposition of "What would I do to make Z_____ a better place to live?", I could have chosen topics from politics to lake enhancement and development, and though these are important, I have chosen two areas that could vastly improve our community. They are health care facilities and attracting manufacturing companies.

D. From the youngest resident to the oldest, health care is of great importance. Right now our closest hospital is 50 miles in any direction. So when an emergency poses a threat, and our only alternative is W____ , the patient's chance of survival, with their deteriorating condition, is reduced. Each year as winter T____s choose to make Z_____ their permanent home, hospital facilities and health care are important factors in their decision-making process. With the construction of a county hospital, those that need special care will know their needs would be met within a reasonable distance.

E. My second area of analysis is through the development of manufacturing companies. By offering short-term tax break incentives, promoting our natural resources of land ripe for development and highlighting our residents as a motivated work force, Z_____ would offer an attractive location for a variety of different manufacturing companies.

F. In my opinion, to improve a community would mean doing what is best for its people.

It is time to realize that of all the valuable capital any community can possess, the most valuable and most decisive is people

E. Presents well-organized evidence to suggest ways to attract manufacturing.

F. Conclusion brings appropriate closure to speech by appealing to values of the audience.

Connections to Standards

Loretta is developing skill in:

● adjusting her use of spoken and written language to communicate effectively with a specific audience for a particular purpose (4).

LORETTA'S PORTFOLIO

Response to Literature (Analysis)

Loretta wrote this piece in response to the following prompt: "Every generation has had its heroes who reflect the general character of their society. Discuss the differences in the concept of the hero in Anglo-Saxon times and today. What do these differences reveal about the change in morals and values? What do they reveal about continuity in our morals and values?" Loretta said she selected this piece for her portfolio because it showed her understanding of the "Beowulf story" and her knowledge of the Norman Schwarzkopf story gained from listening to the news and talking to people. Loretta also states that in this essay she "tried to use a variety of words and had many drafts."

R u b r i c / C o m m e n t a r y

A. Some readers thought the title only partially identifies subject.
B. Attempts to engage reader through use of questions.
C. Has clear thesis sentence.
D. Identifies somewhat superficial similarities between Beowulf/Grendel and Schwarzkopf/Saddam Hussein.

A. Beowulf

B. Heroes. Who are they? How long have they existed? Heroes are described as being people of distinguished courage or ability, admired for their brave deeds and noble qualities. Heroes have existed since the beginning of time, but have been portrayed differently. Beowulf and Norman Schwarzkopf are prime examples

C. to demonstrate the similarities and differences in modern day heroes and Anglo-Saxon heroes.

The stories of Beowulf and General Schwarzkopf are strikingly the same in many ways The two heroes both set out from their countries to help other countries to end war and hate. Beowulf sought out to kill Grendel Grendel was a monster who had

D. been killing men for over 12 years to stay in control of a Mead Hall he had taken reign over. General Schwarzkopf set out to get Sadaam Hussein.

82

A monster of his own, destroying another country for his own wealth and power. They both accomplished their goals through violence, and with much bloodshed peace was brought. This proves our morals and values are very much the same in the sense that we fight for what is right and good.

The Anglo-Saxon hero and

E. our modern day hero have great differences Beowulf was a fictional character who set out to destroy the evil and hate of the world portrayed by Grendel. He chose to attack Grendel one-on-one without any weapons and when his deed was done, in the poem, happiness was restored. On the other hand, General Schwarzkopf's story

F. was actual and his mission was to get and keep Hussein out of Kuwait. His attack was through troops and Sadaam

E. Makes predictable connection between American and Anglo-Saxon values.

F. Identifies somewhat superficial differences (e.g., one is fictional, the other is real) between Beowulf and an actual person. The writer selected a "real" person for the modern example and a fictional hero for the past example. Then the writer compared the two and called the differences a historical development. They may, however, only be a matter of fiction versus "real" differences.

LORETTA'S PORTFOLIO

Paper continued on page 84

G. Simplistic claim not supported by preceding discussion.

H. Conclusion attempts to echo introduction. Introduces points which are not developed or supported in paper. Final sentence lacks specificity.

Connections to Standards

Loretta is developing skill in:

• reading print and nonprint texts to build an understanding of texts and of the cultures of the United States and the world (1);

• comprehending and interpreting texts (2);

• applying knowledge of language structure, language conventions, media techniques, and genre to create print texts (6).

G. was never touched. Though his mission was accomplished, Kuwait will always live in fear. This reveals our differences in morals and values because when we fight for something today many lives are at stake not just a few at a time. Grendel only attacked those who came to "his" Mead Hall, whereas Hussein attacked innocent people and anyone who seemed to get in his way. Today, man has created weapons that can wipe out whole nations for revenge. It seems that back then things were much more "innocent".

H. Heroes. They are people ~~or things~~ everyone seems to need. Beowulf and General Schwarzkof are just ~~a few~~ of the many looked up to. Heroes seem to give people a sense of security as role models. Though heroes have changed over time, the same general concepts never change.

Task

On the entry slip for this piece, Loretta wrote that "the information was gathered from the movie Excalibur and the piece 'Morte d'Arthur.'" She added that this was the first character analysis she had written.

Response to Literature (Character Analysis)

"You will become the land and the land will become you." He who
A. understood the hidden meaning would become true king, was Merlin's explanation to Arthur as to what a king was. Arthur became the bravest and perhaps greatest king ever to rule over medieval Britain. But what is it about Arthur that people admire in him? Perhaps it is through his intriguing background, benevolent actions,
B. or his battle with inner conflict that has made him a legend and kept him alive.

The path that led to Arthur's reign was destiny. King Uther Pendragon fell in love with Igrayne, the Duke of Cornwall's wife. Making a pact with Merlin, Uther took
C. the form of the duke and thus Arthur was conceived. Arthur was raised not knowing of his royal ancestry. But when he released the magic sword from the stone, in which his father had set it, he was proven to be rightful heir to the throne. After pulling out the sword, his step-father and brother knelt, Arthur seeing this replied, "Rise father, for I was your son before I was your king." His step father then told him of his great love for him and turned him down telling Arthur he wasn't his true father and didn't know who was. This showed the love and honesty with which Arthur was raised. Arthur then fought the great knight Juliuns, to regain the throne and when

Rubric / Commentary

A. The writer attempts to engage the reader by opening with a quote and then later using a question to introduce the thesis.

B. The writer advances the analysis by presenting three qualities of character to be discussed.

C. Uses chronology to organize material here. The writer needs to be clear here that "intriguing background" is the first point.

Paper continued on page 86

D. Uses specific incident to support interpretation of Arthur's "intriguing background."

E. Paragraph identifies and discusses Arthur's "benevolent actions," which is second point.

F. Uses quotes appropriately to support interpretation.

G. Paragraph indirectly identifies and discusses Arthur's "inner conflict," but this point needs to be clearly identified as the third point, as the guiding idea in this section.

H. Refers again to Arthur's relationship with the land, but does not explore the meaning of this repeated phrase.

I. Conclusion restates thesis. Final sentence brings appropriate closure.

Connections to Standards

Loretta is developing skill in:

• reading print and nonprint texts to build an understanding of texts and of the cultures of the United States and of the world (1);

• reading literature to build an understanding of the many dimensions of human experience (2);

• applying knowledge of language structure, language conventions, and genre to create and discuss print and nonprint texts (6).

D. he brought him to his mercy, Julius knighted Arthur. And so began the reign of King Arthur.

E. Arthur's considerate and benign character was portrayed through his actions. One of his most famous deeds was the building of the Round Table. He felt all his knights were "noble and equal". The significance for the table was so they would all be "equal" because there was no head or seat of honor. This seemed to make his knights show a great deal more respect and honor for him. Arthur was also quick to admit to his rash reactions. When Arthur is first introduced to Sir Lancelot they fought arrogantly. Arthur used the power of Excalibur to achieve his ambition and broke it in half with his pride and rage. "This excellent knight

F. was meant to win. I used Excalibur to change that verdict. I've lost, I used the ancient sword of my fathers whose power was used to unite all men, not to serve

G. the vanity of a single man."

H. Arthur died fighting with his son. Some believed Arthur had been taken to an imaginary island, Avalon, to be healed. Many felt one day he would return and rule again. The background, actions and inner conflicts faced by Arthur seemed to make him one of the greatest kings that ever lived. Today people are still fascinated by King Arthur and the Knights of the Round Table. And so the tales and Legends of

I. King Arthur will go on being told for many more centuries yet to come.

Task

Loretta's teacher certified that she had read the books listed below. All the titles Loretta listed appear here. An illustrative log entry is also shown.

Reading Logs

"Mindbend" by Robin Cook

This book was about a couple who was trying to have a child and every time she would get pregnant the doctor would tell her that the baby would be born severely retarded and he would highly recommend an abortion. The third time this happened he husband became very worried and suggested she get a second opion as to why this was happening. She doesn't want to and he can't understand why. He goes undercover and finds all of her pregnancies were normal and she was being brain washed. They were using fetal tissue for research. He sets out to stop all the corruption and ends up almost losing his life.

"What a Baby Costs" taken from "The Book of Virtues" by William J. Bennet

"The End of Summer" by Rosamunde Pilcher

Rubric

The requirements for breadth in reading were
- at least twenty-five books (or equivalent);
- a balance of literature and non-literary works;
- at least three different genres or modes;
- at least five different authors;
- at least four books by the same author, in the same genre, or about one topic.

Commentary

In the reading log, Loretta provides a succinct retelling of the plot of a popular novel.
Retellings indicate literal comprehension and possibly some interpretation.

Paper continued on page 88

Commentary

Texts read are not particularly challenging, but indicate that Loretta reads and comprehends a somewhat limited range of materials.
Reading list includes some of the sources used for research project on American criminal justice system.

Connections to Standards

Loretta is developing skill in:

• reading a range of fiction and nonfiction (1).

Ina by: Karen Baker Kletzing

"Animal Farm" Chp. 10
by George Orwell

"Even Prisoners Must Have Hope"
by Richard Stratton   *Newsweek* Oct 17, 1994

"The Rogue's Daughter" by Molly Noble Bull

"Mutation" by Robin Cook

"Chessie's King" by Kathleen Karr

"Little Red Riding Hood" – taken from the
by: James Finn Garner *Politically Correct Bedtime Stories*

Mr. Murderer – by Dean Koonz

U.S. News + World Report, Sept 19, 1994
Battling Deviant Behavior by Erica Good

"A Child's Prayer" – taken from "The Book
by: William J. Bennett   Virtues"

Task

Included here in Loretta's research project are portions of the final paper, a preliminary outline of the paper, and samples of notes taken from various sources. Loretta's records for this project suggest that she drew on background knowledge, that she makes connections among subjects and activities in school, and that she gave considerable attention to sharpening the focus of her paper.

Research Project **Middle**

LORETTA'S PORTFOLIO

THE AMERICAN CRIMINAL JUSTICE SYSTEM

A. Every American has fallen victim to our poorly managed Criminal Justice System; it is hurting us in our pockets and jeapordizing our personal safety. It starts from the time the offender commits the crime and is run through the justice system up until the time they are released back into civilization. It's time to close the door on the current system and move on to open the door that we first intended to open. The American Criminal Justice has failed the society it was designed to protect.

B. From the beginning of time until now, retribution has always been the answer to society's problems. Our Criminal Justice System has historically always used punishment for criminal acts. Pre-Revolutionary forms of punishment included banishment public ridicule, public torture, beatings, brandings, and fines. In our present system time and money are the primary means by which punishment is calculated (H. R. De Luca, "Punishment vs. Rehabilitation" 38).

The four major goals of the American Criminal Justice System are deterrence, punishment, incapacitation, and rehabilitation (H. R. De Luca, "Punishment vs. Rehabilitation" 38). Deterrence is the prevention of criminals to engage in criminal acts. Punishment is causing loss or pain as retribution for a crime. Incapacitation is the prevention of a convict from committing crimes by limiting his ability. Rehabilitation is the changing of a criminals way of thinking so as to diminish his need to engage in criminal activity (one requirement for rehabilitation is that both an alternative means of making a living and of satisfying internal needs must be provided). These four goals have been enveloped

C. into a speculative basic structure for studying a society's response to crime and its handling of criminals.

Sentencing a criminal for a crime are put in ranges set by state legislatures. These ranges are used to determine penalties and usually put in terms of fines or incarceration. The ranges set for a criminal depend on the objectives of the

Rubric / Commentary

A. Engages the reader in the first sentence by appealing to and identifying with the audience's concerns.

B. Reviews history, restates goals, and defines terms, but does not always advance argument.

C. Some awkward sentences interfere with reader's understanding.

Paper continued on page 90

D. Cites facts and statistics about sentencing policies to support initial claim that the American criminal justice system has failed.

E. Effective transition from percentage of criminals who are narcotics offenders to discussion of drug rehabilitation.

F. The connection between the topic sentence "America is crying for harsher punishments in prison" and the anecdote which follows is not clear. However, use of anecdote is appropriate strategy for supporting argument.

G. Demonstrates ability to interpret information.

D. Criminal Justice System, constitutional and statutory limitations, the seriousness of the crime, and characteristics of the criminal (Elyce Zenoff, Encyclopedia of the American Judicial System 915).

Once a lawbreaker has been given a sentence his time is automatically divided into thirds. The first third of sentences are usually served. During the second third the term is served only if parole hasn't been issued. The third part is rarely ever served because it is taken off the sentence for good behavior within prison (Federal Probation, 39). Of all convicted felons only a fraction of them actually ever see a jail.

Statistics indicate that only one-third of all criminals sentenced actually go. The other two-thirds are put on probation. The average time for both murderers and burglars is 16 months behind bars (Editorial Research Reports 435)

What happens to the other two-thirds of convicted felons? They are receiving nothing more than a slap on the hand. Those that do go to prison aren't serving their complete sentences. How can we better the population as a whole or deter crime if we aren't serving the example to society?

Early release and shortened sentences are mostly due to the overcrowding in prisons (Editorial Research Reports 435). Much of the overcrowding resulted from the War on Drugs Boom in the 1980's. Prisons have been stuffed due to the mandatory sentences for minor drug offenses. Of all prisoners, 61% are narcotic offenders (Jill Smolowe, "Throwing Away the Key" 57).

E. It's time we stop using our system for something it can't cure. Drug users need rehabilitation. If prisons don't provide rehabilitation for "Druggies" it will only be a matter of time before they are back into the system again for the same crime. How can we expect addicts to change if we don't show them how. . . .

F. America is crying for harsher punishments in prison. Richard Stratton spent eight years in prison on charges for smuggling drugs. "I was demeaned and scared. I waded through sewage backed up from toilets. I lived in overcrowded cells. I saw men brutally beaten," Stratton describes the prison. He felt that his stay in prison could have been point-

G. less, but he was offered a chance at an education. Despite the harsh realities of prison he had the chance to change his life and he did. He now lives a successful life wife his wife and children. By taking away these opportunities, prisoners can't

H. change the behavior that sent them to crime. (Richard Stratton, "Even Prisoners Need Hope" 89)

Recidivism rates are currently at an all time high. Research indicates that offenders who have been sent to prison have a higher recidivism rate than those placed in alternative forms of punishment (Florida State University Law Review, 493). This proves prisons have neither properly detered criminal activity nor rehabilitated offenders as effectively as alternative options.

If harsh punishment isn't working why aren't our politicians making changes? Alternatives aren't quick and take time to make an overall effect. Politicians want to be on record for getting things done now, since our society cries for vengeance in the wake of all crimes. When re-election time rolls around, politicians want society to see what society wants to see, whether or not the policies worked. So the cycle continues and we all suffer.

Due to the overcrowding in prisons, policy makers are looking into rehabilitation and correction programs. The goals of rehabilitation are to change an offenders character so as to diminish his criminal propensities (Erica Goode, "Battling Deviant Behavior" 74). To create a change in a criminal's thought so committing crime is no longer an ambition or necessity. The National Institute of Mental Health spent a total of $126.5 million dollars on the study of depression and sex offenses. Many of the studies show that pedophiles grew up in strict homes where sexuality was never openly discussed. They overturned many myths that pedophiles were themselves sexually molested ("Battling Deviant Behavior" 76). There is no substantial proof that this was a major contributor to their adult actions.

Scientists began studies using chemical aids. The use of "antidrogen" drugs to curve sex offenders sexual urges and abate their sex drives. Antidepressants are also administered

I. to control a chemical in the brain called serotonin. Researchers are reporting successful results in these studies ("Battling Deviant Behavior" 76).

Another type of rehabilitation is group psychotherapies to help patients face and understand their "sexual paraphilias". "Aversion" therapies give offenders unpleasant stimulus when shown pictures that stimulate them. Training is also given to help criminals better adapt to society.

H. Speculates reasonably about cause of current problem.
I. Information on treatment of sex offenders and group therapy seems to digress from the argument.

LORETTA'S PORTFOLIO

Paper continued on page 92

J. Appropriate conclusion alludes to a nationally known image, references a famous person, and suggests a solution to the problem researched.

K. Conclusion suggests that, through reading, Loretta has arrived at a deeper understanding of her topic ("it's the policies we've enacted in response to crime.").

L. List of works cited shows that Loretta is aware of the importance of giving evidence of sources consulted. The format of the list suggests that Loretta is aware of the importance of using a consistent style for citation.

Connections to Standards

Loretta is developing skill in:

• conducting research on issues; gathering , evaluating, and synthesizing data from a variety of sources; and communicating her discoveries in ways that suit her purpose and audience (7);

• using informational resources to gather and synthesize information (8).

Yet the effects of group therapies seem to disappear once the therapy stops and the offender returns to the general public, where temptation is at its greatest. Even the most progressive forms of rehabilitation provide no elixir and no guarantee.

J. Our criminal justice system can be described as a revolving door. The challenges of our decade should be to improve and perfect our system. Not only for justice, but for the betterment of humankind. Woodrow Wilson once proclaimed "Unless justice be done to others it will not be done

K. to us". It's not essentially crime that's driving the growth or costs of the criminal justice system; it's the policies we've enacted in response to crime.

WORKS CITED

L. De Luca, H.R. "Punishment vs. Rehabilitation" <u>Federal Probation</u> September (1991): 38-39

Zenoff, Elyce. <u>Encyclopedia of the American Justice System</u> Charles Scribner's Sons, New York, 1987: 915

United States Congress. <u>Editorial Research Reports</u> August 1989 Congressional Quarterly Inc. : 435

Smolowe, Jill. "Throwing Away the Key" <u>Time</u> February 1994 55-59

Rideau, Wilbert. "Why Prisons Don't Work" <u>Time</u> March 1994 80

Stratton, Richard. "Even Prisoners Need Hope" <u>Newsweek</u> October 1994 : 89

<u>Florida State University Law Review</u> Winter 1991 : 493

Goode, Erica. "Battling Deviant Behavior" <u>U.S. News and World Report</u> September 1994 : 74-76

Task

The research project is a typical set of entries in a portfolio, including an overall plan for data collection (outline), reading notes from data collection, and, as in Natalie's portfolio (pages 72–75), an interview and observation.

Describe the assignment that prompted this work (attach other pages if necessary):
I was involved in the debate team for   . I already knew a lot of information on this topic, so when a research was assigned I was able to write a well put together paper.

This piece was not only to let me learn a lot on the topic, but I helped to prepare me to write a research in college.
What makes this work good evidence for this entry?
This piece required a lot of research and in doing so I read a vast amount to completely understand my topic. I also read a wide variety of materials to see different views of my topic. In writing my report it had to be perfect and a lot of writing and rewriting took place in completing it.

The American Criminal Justice system has failed the society it was designed to protect.

I INTRODUCTION

II CRIMINAL JUSTICE SYSTEM
   A. History and Today
   B. Major Objectives

III SENTENCING
   A. Ranges
   B. Lengths : Overcrowding
   C. Argument

IV PRISONS
   A. Failures-Harsh Punishment vs. Education
   B. Anecdote
   C. Recidivism
   D. Argument

V ALTERNATIVES-REHABILITATON
   A. Goals
   B. Researches
   C. Types
      1. Chemical Aids
      2. Counseling Therapy
      3. Training
   D. Argument

VI CONCLUSION

Commentary

Outline of paper with thesis sentence written at top. Outline and paper suggest that Loretta can create and follow a logical structure for organization.

Connections to Standards

Loretta is developing skill in:
• using elements of the writing process appropriately (5).

LORETTA'S PORTFOLIO

Commentary

Notes show that Loretta documents sources consulted for later reference. Notes also suggest that she understands how to paraphrase and how to combine information gained from several different sources.

Notes appear almost verbatim in final paper. Inclusion of interesting but irrelevant information suggests that Loretta does not always make discriminating use of texts read.

Connections to Standards

Loretta is developing skill in:

• gathering data from a variety of print texts (7).

Battling Deviant Behavior
US NEWS & WORLD REPORT   SEPT. 19, 1994
by: Erica Goode

The National Institute of Mental Health spent a total of $126.5 million dollars on the study of depression and sex offenders. Many of the studies show that pedophiles grew up in strict homes where sexuality was never openly discussed. They also overturned many myths that pedophiles were themselves sexually molested. There was no proof that this was a major contribution to their adult actions.

Scientists began studies using chemical aids. The use of antiandrogen drugs to curve sex offenders sexual urges and abate their sex drives. Anti-depressants are also administered to control a chemical in the brain called Serotonin. Researchers are reporting successful results in these studies.

Another type of rehab. is group psychotherapies to help patients face and understand their sexual paraphilias. "Aversion" therapies give unpleasant stimulus when an offender is shown pictures that stimulate him. Training is also given to help offenders better adapt to society.

Yet these effects of group therapies fade once the therapy stops and the offender returns to the general public where temptation is at its greatest. In most promising types of rehabilitation provide elixir and no guarantee.

Editorial Research Reports — Aug 11, 1989
pg. 435 — Congressional Quarterly

Statistics indicate that only one-third of all criminals sentenced actually go. The other ⅔ are sentenced to probation.

The avg. time for both murderers and burglars only spend 16 months behind bars. This is mostly due to the overcrowding in prisons. The sentences served are cut into thirds. omit

Task

Students were asked to include in their portfolios examples of multiple drafts on some selections (but not all). Students were asked to use editing and drafting to develop the reading and writing.

Every American has fallen victim to our poorly managed Criminal Justice system: it is hurting us in our pockets and jeapordizing our personal safety. It starts from the time the offender commits the crime and is run through the justice system up until the time they are released back into society. It's time to close the door on the current system and move on to open the door that we first intended to open. Thesis

From the beginning of time till now, retribution has always been the answer to society's problem.

Commentary

In the first paragraph of Loretta's first draft, only minor revisions were made, including a reminder to formulate and state a thesis. Editing did not eliminate error in agreement of pronoun and antecedent.

Our criminal Justice has historically always used punishment for criminal acts. Pre-Revolutionary forms of punishment included banishment, public ridicule, public torture, beatings, brandings, and fines

In our present system time

Commentary

Another excerpt from first draft illustrates lack of revision and only minor editing.

Connections to Standards

Loretta is developing skill in:

• using different writing process elements appropriately (5).

LORETTA'S PORTFOLIO

Summary Commentary of Loretta's Portfolio

Loretta's portfolio shows that she is making progress toward adequate levels of achievement in English language arts. The artifacts presented here suggest that Loretta has good encoding skills. There are some errors in mechanics and usage in finished pieces, such as the character analysis of King Arthur and "The American Criminal Justice System." Although these errors are somewhat distracting, they do not cause confusion about meaning. Loretta's writing is often fluent, but there are signs that she is still developing her "academic" style. In the character analysis of King Arthur, for example, some words are used oddly and some constructions are awkward: (1) "his battle with inner conflict . . ."; (2) "When Arthur is first introduced to Sir Lancelot they fought arrogantly."

Evidence of Loretta's readings shows that she is a fluent reader of popular fiction and nonfiction, but rarely tackles challenging literary or informational texts. Her log entries show that she can summarize the plots of the texts she reads, but she needs to develop analytical, critical, and evaluative skills. Her paper on the American criminal justice system also gives evidence that Loretta reads and understands a variety of informational texts.

The artifacts in Loretta's portfolio suggest that although she is developing skills in processing information, she still uses a limited repertoire of strategies for understanding and representing ideas. For example, although Loretta claims to have done a lot of re-writing, little evidence of that claim appears in her portfolio. Drafts reflect only minor, editorial changes. Her reflective essay introducing the portfolio is brief and discusses strengths, weaknesses, and accomplishments in very general terms. One judge who scored Loretta's portfolio wrote

> Self-evaluation remains almost entirely at the surface level, stating things like "a lot of writing and rewriting took place in completing it," but doing little to explain the nature of that writing and rewriting.

Loretta's portfolio contains several examples of her ability to locate and use information, but she is not yet a skilled manipulator of informational texts. It is difficult to tell from the artifacts in Loretta's portfolio what strategies she uses to read and to interpret challenging literature. One judge who scored Loretta's portfolio wrote

> King Arthur characterization is more a plot summary than critical analysis. Beowulf . . . piece also doesn't elaborate as successfully and fully as might be expected.

Throughout the paper on the American criminal justice system, Loretta cites the sources of the many facts and statistics she has included, and works cited are listed at the end of the paper. "The American Criminal Justice System," probably the strongest piece in the portfolio, indicates that Loretta has mastered some aspects of the forms and functions of reading and writing for research, but she is still learning many of the basics in secondary school research projects. Judges who scored Loretta's portfolio commented that she produced an "adequate synthesis" of source texts in the final document. One judge wrote

> Uses a significant number of public documents to put together a substantial report of information, which demonstrates a substantial understanding of the issues. However, the use of the information doesn't yet reach the point of being insightful or effective, but certainly approaches it.

Loretta's portfolio pieces suggest that she has a well-developed personal voice, but has not written for a range of close and distant audiences. For example, in the text of the speech on improving her hometown, Loretta connects strongly to a real audience: "Though a small town, it is where most of us have grown up and where our memories of childhood will always dwell. This is our home." A similar voice can be heard in "The American Criminal Justice System," which was influenced by Loretta's debate club experience. One judge who scored Loretta's portfolio commented that her speeches are her "strongest writing." The pieces in which Loretta addresses a distant audience are less successful. For example, in the "Beowulf" piece, Loretta's introduction sounds contrived: "Heroes. Who are they? How long have they existed? Heroes are described as being people of distinguished courage or ability, admired for their brave deeds and noble qualities." Throughout the piece, Loretta attempts to adopt an authoritative voice. This often leads to either convoluted sentences, unconvincing claims, or a vague gesture toward a point: (1) "This reveals our differences in morals and values because when we fight for something today many lives are at stake not just a few at a time"; (2) "Today, man has created weapons that can wipe out whole nations for revenge. It seems that back then things were much more 'innocent.'" We have to celebrate Loretta's efforts here, but we also need to note where help is needed.

Loretta's portfolio selections suggest that she is developing control of persuasive and informational writing. The "Community Improvement" speech shows that she understands persuasion quite well (e.g., establishing a common bond with the audience). Her attempts at literary analysis (e.g., the character analysis of King Arthur and the comparison of Beowulf and Schwarzkopf) suggest that her understanding of disciplinary concepts (e.g., "character," "hero") and her ability to construct and elaborate on literary interpretations are still developing. The selections in Loretta's portfolio show that she does know something about some key concepts in English. For example, she demonstrates some understanding of character in the pieces on Beowulf and King Arthur. "The American Criminal Justice System" shows that Loretta has a fairly sophisticated understanding of issues underlying reform of the criminal justice system. However, for the most part, Loretta's understanding of cultural themes and ideas needs to be developed.

Overall, Loretta's portfolio demonstrates that she has a high level of conceptual knowledge (knowing that), but that she is still learning how to put that knowledge to use (knowing how). For example, Loretta knows that paragraphs should begin with topic sentences, but she has not yet mastered the skill of writing effective topic sentences. She demonstrates that she understands the function of conclusions, and hers are generally appropriate. Evidence of Loretta's background knowledge (knowing about) is sparse. Her writing usually follows a formulaic approach (e.g., five-paragraph essay). She is skillful at using the voice and rhetorical devices of editorial writing, but does not provide evidence of knowing about other voices or other genres. Her reading lacks breadth (notably absent is evidence of reading other than contemporary works) and depth (background reading for research paper is primarily popular press). Loretta's portfolio places her work in the middle range of performance. It provides a good foundation from which she may expand her repertoire of processes and content.

Portfolios

Natalie

Loretta

Terry

Terry compiled this portfolio at the end of his ninth-grade year. His portfolio represents a selection of the work he completed over the course of the school year. We have selected only some pieces from Terry's portfolio for inclusion here.

Task

Terry's Table of Contents appears below. Not all of the entries listed in the Table of Contents appear here.

Table of Contents

Low

Table of Contents

Entry Name   #

Letter of introduction   #1

Student Response Booklet   #2

Edgar Allan Poe Composition   #3

"My Friend Ben   #4

Cherokee Composition   #5

"Uniforms"   #6

"Movie Review"   #7

Writing Reflection   #8

Tail of 2 cities Essay   #9

Reading Reflection   #10

Reflective Essay (Letter)

Rubric / Commentary

A. In this sparse letter of introduction, Terry makes vague statements about his work.
B. He makes the simple connection that his best pieces arose from texts he enjoyed writing and reading, while his worst pieces were linked to "the things I thought was boring."
C. Noticeable usage, spelling, and capitalization errors occur here and continue throughout the portfolio.

Task

Many portfolios require a reflective essay (letter of introduction) to review strengths and weaknesses in the portfolio.

A.

> Letter Of introduction
>
> The reason I chose these 10 peices to go into my portfolio is I think they represent my better work over the cource of the school year. these where on some of the things that I enjoyed to write and read over the school year. I think that my better peices are the ones that I enjoyed to do. my worst things would probably be the things I thought was boring.

B.

C.

Connections to Standards

Terry needs to show substantial improvement in:

● adjusting written language to communicate effectively with a specific audience for a particular purpose (4).

Argument

Rubric / Commentary

A. Inconsistent use of capitalization.
B. This brief paragraph suggests that Terry has understood some of what he read (probably a U.S. History text) about Jackson's treatment of the Cherokee. However, his response to the question he raises seems incomplete and the final sentence leaves the reader wondering how Terry defines the term "democracy."

Task

On the entry slip for this piece Terry wrote, "I chose this peice to go in because I like to read on stuff like this so it was easy to wright on."

A.

> The cherokee tried desperately to protect the constitution, but failed. Does the Trail of Tears then represent a failier of American democracy? Yes the Cherokee helped Jackson fight aginst the creek Indians and they obayed the constitution but as soon as Jackson became president he wanted them removed to the land West of the Mississippi river. This would show that the democracy has failed because it is going against its all's.

B.

Connections to Standards

Terry needs to show substantial improvement in:

● applying a wide range of strategies to comprehend and interpret texts (3).

Task

On the entry slip for this piece Terry explained that he chose it for his portfolio "because this is on something I enjoyed to watch not something I had to."

> ### The Lion King
>
> A. Simba was the main character in The movie he was born into a kingdon his father was the king but he was killed by his brother scar. Simba ran away because he thought he killed his father when he was gone he met pumba and
> B. timone. When he came back his Home was runed by his uncles ruling then Simba faught his uncle and won the ruling
> C. of the land him and nala had a little cub at the end of the movie.

Rubric / Commentary

A. This very literal and incomplete plot summary suggests that Terry understood some of what he viewed. He understands the concept of "main character," and recalls the names of other prominent characters. He seems to want to analyze the main character but slips into plot summary.

B. There is no evidence of substantive interpretation.

C. As a piece of writing, this sparse "review" lacks any attempt to engage or sustain the reader's interest, to evaluate the visual text, or to express an opinion about it.

Task

On the entry slip for this piece, Terry wrote, "I chose this piece for my portfolio because I got to put what I want on it. It was from what I think not from something I have no idea about."

> Edger Alan Poe would not have been
> A. such a great writer had his life not been so tragic. Every time a person he loved died he would write something that delt with this and It usually became
> B. famous. he had alot of isperation because alot of people died that he loved and he thought that the worst thing that could happen is a buityful woman d,jay. he was also inspired to wright when his wife was sick which was for 5 years
> C. then when she died he wrote another poem.

Rubric / Commentary

A. A strong topic sentence which is supported by some evidence. Terry is making a good attempt at generalizing.

B. Facts used to support claim are generally accurate, although the cause-effect relationship is not clearly analyzed.

C. Piece lacks conclusion. It simply ends.

Connections to Standards

Terry needs to show substantial improvement in:

• comprehending, interpreting, and evaluating texts (3);

• applying knowledge of language structure, language conventions, and genre to create and discuss print and nonprint texts (6).

Breadth of Reading

Low

Task

Terry states personal criteria for reading–books that are "good," poems that "rhyme and sound good," and "mystery and horor or any kind of book where something is going on." Interestingly, neither mystery nor horror are represented on the list of books he includes here.

Rubric

The student was asked to present evidence that he or she had read
- at least twenty-five books (or equivalent);
- a balance of literature and non-literary public discourse;
- at least three different genres or modes;
- at least five different authors;
- at least four books about one issue.

Commentary

The range of reading is extremely limited, consisting of assigned reading plus some reading in popular magazines. Such a brief listing does not hint at how well Terry understands what he reads or what his preferences are.

The book log may be telling us quite clearly that Terry has serious problems in his reading. He is not as fluent as he should be.

The organization of the evidence is inadequate.

Connections to Standards

Terry needs to show substantial improvement in:

• reading a wide range of print and nonprint texts (1);

• reading a wide range of literature (2).

Reading Reflection

I like to read diffrent things mostly magazines and newspapers. But I also like to read books. but the books have to be good. I don't like to read romantic books or poetry but I do like poems that ryme and sound good I also like to read things like mystery and horor or any kind of book where something is going on. Some of the things I have read this year: "federico falcon" romio and juilet Tail of 2 cities, Ichosay Jaamain, "the Decameron" "meditation 17" Sports Allistrated, Game News, TV Guid 2 social Studies books, Where the red fern grows and some poetry

Task

On the entry slip for this piece Terry wrote, "I chose this page to put in my portfolio because I enjoyed reading this it was not boring and it was very easy to wright on and I accutally injoyed wrighting on this book." The title of the piece appears in the Table of Contents but not on the piece itself.

Response to Literature (Character Analysis)

A. SYDNEY CARTON IS DIFFRENT THAN CHARLES DARNAY IN MANY WAYS. CHARLES DARNAY IS EVERYTHING THAT SYDNEY CARTON COULD HAVE BEEN. CHARLES DARNAY IS A VERY WELL DRESSED AND VERY SUCCESSFUL IN HIS WORK, BUT C.J. STRYVER GETS ALL THE CREDIT FOR WHAT SYDNEY CARTON DOES. CHARLES DARNAY HAS LUCIE, BUT SYDNEY CARTON LOVES HER.

B. THERE ARE MANY REASONS THAT SYDNEY CARTON WISHES HE COULD BE LIKE CHARLES DARNAY. CHARLES IS A WELL DRESSED, CLEAN PERSON THAT IS A VERY SUCCESSFUL TUTOR. SYDNEY CARTON IS DRUNK ALOT OF THE TIME, HE IS NOT CLEAN, HIS CLOTHS ARE A MESS AND HE IS ALWAYS MORE INTERESTED IN HIS WORK THAN ANYTHING ELSE. SYDNEY CARTON ACTS LIKE HE WANTS TO KEEP TO HIMSELF SYDNEY CARTON AND CHARLES DARNAY ARE NOT VERY GOOD FRIENDS IN THE BOOK SYDNEY CARTON SAIS TO CHARLES DARNAY "DO YOU
C. THINK I PARTICULARLY LIKE YOU?"

D. ANOTHER THING THAT SEPERATES CHARLES DARNAY FROM SYDNEY CARTON IS LUCIE. CHARLES DARNAY AND LUCIE ARE IN LOVE AND SYDNEY CARTON CAN'T HAVE HER THAT IS WHY SYDNEY CARTON SAYS HE DOESN'T LIKE CHARLES DARNAY. SYDNEY CARTON SAID "IF ONLY THOSE EYES LOOKED AT ME LIKE THEY LOOK AT YOU". HE IS MEANING THAT HE WISHES THAT SHE WOULD LOOK AT HIM AND LOVE
E. HIM LIKE SHE LOVES CHARLES DARNAY. CHARLES DARNAY IS ALSO
F. VERY SUCCESSFUL AND LUCIE WOULD BE BETTER OFF WITH HIM THAN WITH SYDNEY CARTON THE ONLY THING THAT THEY BOTH HAVE IN
G. COMMON IS THEY BOTH CARE FOR LUCIE.

Rubric / Commentary

A. Opens with a clear thesis statement, which is developed with many details.
B. Details show some understanding of plot and character. Begins to suggest interpretation ("Charles Darnay is everything that Sydney Carton could have been."), but does not develop it.
C. Terry quotes from text to support claim about character.
D. The last paragraph adequately discusses the triangle among Lucie, Carton, and Darnay. Again, Terry has selected an appropriate quote to support his claim.
E. The paragraph ends appropriately, but there is no closure for the essay as a whole.
F. Note that Terry's use of all upper-case font disguises his problems with capitalization.
G. This paper represents an advance over much of what we have seen.

Connections to Standards

Terry is developing skill in:

- adjusting his written language to communicate effectively (4);

- applying knowledge of language structure and language conventions to create and discuss print texts (6).

T a s k

Most portfolios attempt to capture evidence of the writer's editing and drafting strategies and habits. In Terry's portfolio we get some samples of this editing and drafting process during the preparation of the analysis of *Tale of Two Cities*.

C o m m e n t a r y

Terry has made some effective revisions between this first draft and his final draft. For example, he has changed the sentence, "Darnay is everything that Carton wishes he was" to the more formal, "Charles Darnay is everything Sydney Carton could have been." He has clarified the rest of this paragraph, omitting the speculation that "Carton probably could have had Lucie if he wasn't allways drunk and in his work."

The second paragraph of this draft is more accurate and better organized in the final paper.

Terry has eliminated many of his errors in conventions in the final draft.

C o n n e c t i o n s t o S t a n d a r d s

Terry is developing skill in:

• using elements of the writing process appropriately (5).

Sydney Carton is diffrent than Charles Darnay in many ways. Darnay is everything that Carton wishes he was Darnay is well dressed and very sucessful Although Carton is a verdy good lawyer he still doesn't get much of the createt most of the createt goes to C.J. Stryver. and Darney has Lucie and Carton wishes he could have her. Carton probably could have had Lucie if he wasen't allways drunk and in his work.

There are many reasons Carton Wishes he was like Darney. Darney is a well dressed clean person that is verry sucesfule darnay is drunk alot not clean and always more interested in his work than anything. Even though he doesn't get much credit for it most of the credit goes to C.J. Stryver. Darney is also wealthy that is not how carton is he is more of a loner that stays to himself instead of mixing with people but Darney is a people person that gets along with everyone Carton also doesn't like Darney he says that in the book "Do you think I particulaly likeyou" he says.

Task

Portfolios often require students to reflect on their work. In this case, the student is being asked to reflect on his writing.

Reflective Essay

Low

Wrighting Reflection

I don't mind wrighting to people where I can talk about real things that happen, and they will wright back. I don't mind wrighting about books that I have read, But I don't like wrighting about fiction. I don't like wrighting about topics that people just give you, and you have no idea about.

Summary Commentary of Terry's Portfolio

Terry's portfolio shows that he needs to make substantial improvement in order to reach adequate levels of achievement in the English language arts. The pieces in Terry's portfolio lack substance. Most consist of one paragraph, the longest being three paragraphs. Terry has given readers little evidence on which to base their judgments of what he knows and can do.

The frequent and distracting errors which pervade the portfolio suggest that Terry has difficulty with encoding. The brief, superficial responses to reading suggest that he has only a limited and literal understanding of what he reads and/or views. An exception is his response to *A Tale of Two Cities,* which suggests that Terry can put forth an interpretation of literature he reads. Judges who scored Terry's portfolio called this piece his "strongest selection." Although he states clear preferences about what he likes to read, Terry has shown little evidence that he is a fluent reader. In writing, Terry applies many rules of usage haphazardly, if at all. Numerous errors in spelling, punctuation, and capitalization are apparent. The "Tail of 2 Cities Essay," however, does suggest that Terry's work benefits from proofreading.

The artifacts in Terry's portfolio suggest that he lacks skill in processing information and that he may not be aware of strategies he might use to better understand and represent ideas. His letter of introduction and entry slips all reinforce his claim that he likes to read and write some things and not others, but he shows minimal awareness as to why this may be so. He does not express the desire to become a better reader or writer and makes no claims about the quality of his reading and writing. He equates good work with work he enjoyed doing—a very basic level of understanding of his own literacy. The evidence of reading presented here suggests that Terry approaches and responds to all texts in similar fashion. The limited evidence of reading suggests he may do very little reading. He seems to have the basic processing skills, but he may not be fluent, given his limited practice.

The portfolio pieces shown here were not written for a range of close and distant audiences. There is only a minimal attempt to engage or sustain reader interest—most pieces simply start and stop. This apparent lack of purpose and awareness of audience gives Terry's brief texts a monotonous quality. Terry does not write in a variety of forms. Each piece (with one exception) consists of a single paragraph, and each paragraph is approximately the same length—as if Terry were following some self-imposed limit on form. Even the longest piece, "A Tail of 2 Cities Essay," consists of three paragraphs— each of approximately the same length as the others. The reader perceives no difference in structure, style, or tone among the Cherokee essay, the *Lion King* review, and the Poe biographical sketch.

The evidence in Terry's portfolio suggests that he has a limited understanding of key concepts in English. For example, in "The Lion King" he identifies Simba as the "main character," but does not pursue this observation. The analysis of *A Tale of Two Cities* shows that Terry does recognize and can explore aspects of character and plot, but this level of analysis is lacking in most of his other work. While some topics suggest cultural ideas Terry might explore (e.g., the failure of democracy for the Cherokee people, issues of use and abuse of power in *The Lion King*), these ideas generally go unexamined.

Overall, Terry's portfolio demonstrates that he has a low level of conceptual knowledge (knowing that). And what he knows, he applies inconsistently. For example, he spells "writing" correctly sometimes and incorrectly ("wrighting") at others. The lack of variety among the artifacts in the portfolio (even though a variety of artifacts was required by the portfolio program in which he participated) suggest that Terry's performance knowledge (knowing how) is also at a low level. Similarly, there is little evidence to suggest that Terry has drawn on background knowledge (knowing about) in order to produce the pieces shown here. In fact, he does not use his personal experiences for supporting detail and helpful guidance.

Terry's case raises interesting questions. He obviously knows what he likes and doesn't like about reading and writing. Since he claims to enjoy reading mystery and horror, why are there no artifacts that reflect that interest? He could have selected books he likes. He claims to have enjoyed viewing *The Lion King,* yet his response to this film is as flat as his other pieces of writing. Why is this so? Yes, we know the obvious explanations and guesses. But we need for Terry to tell us more about what is going on. He claims not to like romantic books or writing about fiction, but at the same time he claims to have enjoyed reading and writing about *A Tale of Two Cities.* What strategies might help Terry move beyond his one-paragraph writing style? Judges who scored Terry's portfolio perceived that "the student put forth a nice effort" and had "a lot of pride in his self-evaluation." But he seems unaware of what he must do to produce an adequate performance. How could Terry be helped to build upon these strengths and to create a portfolio that reflects more breadth and depth? More personal experience writing might help get the flow going and allow him to try different approaches without fear of losing control of his subject. And more drafting and editing-group experience might help him internalize the voices of other readers and writers. In any case, he needs specific guidance and assistance for improvement.

Conclusion

The *Standards Exemplar Series* is the third part of the NCTE standards project: (1) *Standards for the English Language Arts* (NCTE/IRA); (2) the *Standards in Practice* series and the *Standards Consensus* series; and (3) the *Standards Exemplar Series*. The aim of the *Standards Exemplar Series* is the same as that of *Standards for the English Language Arts* (NCTE/IRA, 1996): "to ensure that all students develop the literacy skills they need to succeed in school and in various areas of life" (p. 68). The exemplars and portfolios in this book are intended to make visible to all stakeholders in the educational process the kinds of tasks teachers of English language arts value, the levels of performance that frequently co-exist in a single classroom, and the criteria by which student performances are often evaluated.

It is unfortunate, but true, that many teachers of English language arts still carry on their work in isolation from a professional community and rarely see work by students other than their own. Likewise, many students in English language arts classrooms lack opportunities to study and discuss the work of other students in other classrooms and to evaluate their own performance with reference to standards and/or rubrics. The intent of this book is to put the exemplars and portfolios into the hands of those who stand to benefit most from them—teachers and students.

Three final caveats are in order. (1) Use this book to develop your own local assessment, not as a substitute for it; (2) Use this book as a resource to develop your own course outline, not as *the* course outline; and (3) Use this book to develop your own exemplars, rubrics, and commentaries. Teachers at the local level need to work together to determine how they rank student work.

This book is only a bare sketch of what there is to know about the performance levels of students on the NCTE/IRA standards. The value of this book will be in the processes it generates and the discussions it inspires about what we, the English language arts teaching profession, K–12, value in student work.

Appendix

The tasks in the Appendix show additional ways to assess *Public Discourse, Discussion, Dialogue, Sentence Structure,* and *Conventions.* Some of the tasks include samples of student work, others are simply a description of the task. The selections do not include all the scoring guides—rubrics, exemplars, and/or commentaries.

Task 1: Analysis of Public Discourse

The following task was developed by the College Board as an end-of-year assessment for 12th graders. Students were given one hour to complete the task. Teachers who have used this task have often supplemented the materials below with a map of Napoleon's march and a background summary of Napoleon's life. This task focuses on Standard 3.

READING TASK

Study the following announcements which appeared in the *Moniteur* of France in March, 1815, on Napoleon's march from Elba to Paris. Then respond to the tasks which follow.

March 9: "The monster has escaped from the place of his banishment. . . ."

March 10: "The Corsican ogre has landed at Cape Juan."

March 11: "The tiger has shown himself at Gap. The troops are advancing on all sides to arrest his progress. He will conclude his miserable adventure by becoming a wanderer among the mountains. . . ."

March 12: "The monster has actually advanced as far as Grenoble."

March 13: "The tyrant is now at Lyon. Fear and terror seized all at his appearance."

March 18: "The usurper has ventured to approach to within 60 hours' march of the capital."

March 19: "Bonaparte is advancing by forced marches, but it is impossible he can reach Paris."

March 20: "Napoleon will arrive under the walls of Paris tomorrow."

March 21: "The Emperor Napoleon is at Fontainebleau."

March 22: "Yesterday evening His Majesty the Emperor made his public entry and arrived at the Tuileries. Nothing can exceed the universal joy."

WRITING TASK

Students were asked to respond to the following tasks in writing:

Part 1: "The art of good reporting lies in the willingness to stick to statements of fact."

(a) Identify by their dates any of the ten announcements from the *Moniteur* that, in your judgment, exemplify the above definition of good reporting.

(b) Identify by its date *one* of the ten announcements that, in your judgment, violates the definition of good reporting. Then rewrite this one announcement so as to make it conform to the given definition of good reporting.

Part 2: Show fully and specifically how the succession of epithets (names) applied to Napoleon serves as a key to the changes of mind and heart that must have gone on in the office of the *Moniteur* between March 9 and March 22. To do this you will need to comment on the meanings, the implications, the emotional effects of each one of the epithets.

Part 3: In the manner of the *Moniteur,* write the announcement that might have appeared on or about March 15. Take special care to select a suitable epithet for Napoleon.

Part 4: Comment on the effectiveness of each of the following words or groups of words for achieving the *Moniteur's* purpose of producing certain effects upon its readers and evoking from them certain responses.
(a) March 11: "miserable adventure"
(b) March 12: "actually"
(c) March 13: "all"
(d) March 18: "ventured"
(e) March 22: "Nothing can exceed the universal joy."

Following are sample answers and explanations of how responses were scored.

PART 1 (A)

Exemplar High

March 21 is the only date that exemplifies the given definition of good reporting.
(The readers rated *high* only an answer which gave this single date.)

Exemplar Middle

The readers rated as *middle* the double entry: *March 20, March 21*. This answer recognizes the one factual entry but misses the fact that the March 20 entry is dealing with the future and is therefore not factual.

Exemplar Low

All other answers were rated as *low,* even ones that included in their listing the correct date of March 21.

PART 1 (B)

Exemplar High/Middle

Since *March 21* was the only choice which would not do for this question, the readers gave credit only to answers which in their revised entries did a complete job of deleting everything but fact. The two following samples illustrate a competent handling of this question.
March 19: Bonaparte is advancing toward the walls of Paris.
March 20: Napoleon is en route to the capital.

Exemplar Low

Here are two of the many responses rated *low.*
March 13: The tyrant is now at Lyon. Many were seized with terror at his appearance.
March 11: The tiger (fierce Napoleon) has shown himself at Gap.

PART 2

Exemplar High

The editors of this paper exploit the many connotations which have grown up around a word. For instance, on March 9, when the news of Napoleon's escape from Elba reaches the *Moniteur,* ther is little belief that he will try to retake Paris: his presence "on the loose" out in the Mediterranean somewhere is rather vaguely frightening, like that of some monster of the deep which everyone fears but no one expects to see, than specifically threatening like that of an enemy general about to march on a city. Thus, imagery associated with horror, fantasy, and superstition expresses a vague, indefinable fear.

But when Napoleon lands at Cape Juan, he is a real but far-off threat—a man-eater, posing the specific danger of consuming his compatriots. But, though all at the *Moniteur* recognize that he has *some* power, they feel themselves above this mere foreigner. He cannot possibly eat them. The use of a national label, as often in our language, shows contempt.

On March 11, the journalists recognize that Bonaparte has in fact been capable of doing some damage. They show for the first time an open twinge of fear as manifested in the image of a beast all men fear. Bonaparte is definitely a savage opponent, but still a beast—a tiger, a smart beast, but less than human. This impudent creature must be punished before he begins to think his ability is greater than they hope it is.

The reiteration on the next day of "monster" has not the same significance of fanciful superstition as the first use of the word; now it represents the terrible transition from beast, from mere creature of force, to a shrewd, conniving human being: perhaps this creature is not so far below them. Yet the Parisians stll have difficulty realizing that the danger they thought they had crushed could push itself up once more.

By March 13, the newsmen of Paris are truly afraid—yet they still show their indignation. The word tyrant, so often used in protest literature, has no connotation of authority: his power in the land is as fleeting, though as terrible as his might. The *Moniteur* has every intention of protesting this power.

But the change of heart brought about by almost a week of evidence of Napoleon's strength is apparent in the use of the word "usurper." The editors of the *Moniteur* are contemplating living under Napoleon's rule. For while the word "usurper" implies an unjust seizure of power, it also implies a real legal control, backed up by the instruments of government, and fairly permanent.

There is a real chance that Bonaparte will take Paris now. By the 19th though the editors are not fond of the Corsican, they realize that it is better not to throw dirty names at him and risk winning his disfavor.

During the course of the previous day, the editors have decided that if one must be polite, one might as well be cordial. They are now ready to accept Napoleon's entrance to Paris as inevitable and are willing to call him by his first name.

During the next two days, the officials at the *Moniteur* decide to ride on top of the times, instead of merely with them, but at least it does take two days for them to work up to a really glowing appellation for the former ogre. Perhaps even in the most expedient men there is a certain inertia to hypocrisy.

Exemplar Middle

Upon Napoleon's escape from Elba, the *Moniteur*, a royalist paper at the time, referred to the ex-emperor as a "monster." A day later he became the "Corsican ogre." In Paris, the editor was busy thinking of vitriolic epithets to heap upon Napoleon until opposition to the Imperial cause began to crumble and the "Corsican ogre" troops approached the cities of France.

Gentler names were then used by the *Moniteur.* The "tyrant" became a "usurper". All implications of misrule were gone from the paper's pages. On March 19, the ex-Emperor became "Bonaparte" and the next day the *Moniteur* was on a first name basis, calling him "Napoleon." Realizing that the "Corsican ogre" was about to conquer Paris, the paper suddenly began to call him "Emperor," and when he entered the city, greeted him as "His Majesty."

Exemplar Low

Within a period of two weeks, the *Moniteur* changed in its regard of Napoleon from calling him a "monster" to proclaiming him "His Majesty the Emperor." As Napoleon drew nearer to his goal, the people became increasingly more used to his presence. At first, a rebel, a fanatic with strange methods, he became, in people's minds, a liberator of sorts.

PART 3

Exemplar High

The Corsican agitator has somehow penetrated beyond the boundaries of Lyon.

Exemplar Middle

The oppressor has forced his way into Central France. He has received very little aid in his venture.

Exemplar Low

The unleashed lioness nears the city walls ready to pounce.

PART 4 (A)

Exemplar High

"Miserable adventure" immediately classifies Napoleon's triumphal return as a half-baked, futile attempt to regain an empire which was lost long ago. These words are well chosen and convey a set image to the reader. The *Moniteur* wishes, through these words, to make the Parisians pity the vain efforts of an old man and therefore to minimize the possible chance of the populace of Paris joining him by holding Napoleon's endeavors up for scorn.

Exemplar Middle

The phrase "miserable adventure" seems to state that there is no possibility of this move of Napoleon's having any great effect on politics or being any more than an "adventure." The fact that it has no hope of progressing makes it miserable.

Exemplar Low

The effectiveness given of "miserable adventure," has a purpose of producing an effect that Napoleon didn't care anymore and the whole thing turned out wrong.

PART 4 (B)

Exemplar High

By using the word "actually" in the announcement of March 12, the *Moniteur* manages to evoke a tone of disbelief. To the people, it would seem nearly impossible that Napoleon could advance as far as Grenoble. Once again, by using a word which brings about a tone of disbelief, the *Moniteur* has managed to make the people laugh a little at the absurd daring of Napoleon.

Exemplar Middle

This word makes it appear as if Napoleon is lucky that he got as far as he did and that it was almost impossible for him to go any farther.

Exemplar Low

I do not think actually is effective enough. It implies that they cannot believe how Napoleon could possibly be capable of advancing as far as Grenoble. If he is still considered a monster, then his accomplishment should not surprise them.

PART 4 (C)

Exemplar High

In claiming that terror seized *all* at Lyon, the editors seek to establish that Napoleon is receiving no popular support and that the people as one body hate and fear him. Readers would infer that because all at Lyon are terrified, Napoleon is a cruel and tyrannical despot, a madman without pity.

Exemplar Middle

"All" is a strong, overwhelming term, designed to show the complete terror instilled by Napoleon's appearance.

Exemplar Low

"All" here means the entire populus, evoquing sentiments of pride and power.

PART 4 (D)

Exemplar High

The announcement of March 18 once more emphasizes Napolion's temerity in daring to advance so brazenly through France. "He ventures," says the incredulous Moniteur, and its subsribers consequently wonder what right has he. *Ventures* implies that, in daring to progress so far, Napoleon will incur some fatal catastrophe for his rash boldness.

Exemplar Middle

"Ventured" indicates that he is surprisingly daring to attempt such an impossible task.

Exemplar Low

"Ventured" connotes the apparent docility of Napoleon. For this reason the *Moniteur* quickly takes his side and praises him.

PART 4 (E)

Exemplar High

"Nothing can exceed the universal joy." Like the sound of beating on a hollow barrel or the pounding of fists against a great stone wall, these words are false, hollow, and ineffectual. Anyone who had been reading "Le Moniteur" would know what hypocrital bosh this statement was. It sounds more like a frantic effort to save the editor's skin than an attempt to accomplish any particular effect.

Exemplar Middle

The Moniteur is subtly letting all know that they had better be joyful. Everyone else was, or should be, and it was not wise to be otherwise.

Exemplar Low

"Nothing can exceed the universal joy" shows that virtually everyone is happy. The staff of the *Moniteur* weren't strictly keeping with the facts, but they didn't care. They were happy.

T a s k 2: Discussion of Literature

The following task was developed by the College Board for use with 9th and 10th graders. This task was designed to extend over several class periods. In one variation, the College Board task was modified so that the teacher could assess discussion skills. This task focuses on Standards 1 and 2.

Students read the poem "My Last Duchess" by Robert Browning. (The text is widely available.) The teacher may need to supply some background material before the students read the poem. Students may need to know that the story takes place in Renaissance Italy in the sixteenth century. Students may also need to know the marriage customs of the time, e.g., "dowry." The teacher may wish to comment on the relationship existing between the Renaissance nobleman and the artist. Students will need to know what a dramatic monologue is: in this kind of poem only one person speaks, though the reader can deduce from what gets said who is listening and what is happening. The students need to see that the poet is limited to a single person's speech as a means of defining character, implying dramatic action, and usually indicating the presence of an audience. Comparing the restrictions of this form to the freedoms of the short story might help students understand some of the differences of form. Finally, the students may need definitions of the following words:

officious: meddlesome, line 27
lessoned: taught a lesson, line 40
munificence: generosity, line 49
disallowed: refuse, line 51
avowed: admitted openly, confessed frankly, line 52

QUESTIONS FOR CLASS DISCUSSION

1. You have been told that the setting for this poem is Renaissance Italy, in the sixteenth century. What details in the poem establish this setting?
2. Who is the speaker in the poem? To whom is he speaking and how do you know?
3. In what part of the palace are the speaker and his visitor when the poem begins? Where have they been and where are they going? What business is being transacted and how do you know?
4. The word "Frà" (in lines 3, 6, and 16) refers to a monk and means "brother." How does the Duke feel toward Frà Pandolph and how do you know? What do these feelings reveal about the Duke?
5. How do you account for the Duke's being able to state so fluently what Frà Pandolph probably said to the Duchess while he was painting her portrait?
6. What does the Duke reveal about himself when he says he is the only one to draw the curtain covering his wife's picture? (lines 9–10)
7. What further indications of the Duke's character do you discover in the phrase "if they durst," line 11?
8. In lines 13–34 the Duke paints a portrait in words of his "last Duchess" in which he states the reasons for his displeasure with her. In picturing the Duchess, however, he also presents the reader with a portrait of himself. What qualities of his character do you discover through what he says about the Duchess?
9. In lines 34–43 the Duke explains why he never told his wife that she displeased him. What do these reasons tell us about his character?
10. In line 45 the Duke says, "I gave commands." What do you think these commands were? What makes you think so? Should the poem have told you instead of leaving you to guess?
11. What do lines 49–54 suggest about the size of the dowry the Duke is expecting from his next Duchess? Is the Duke sincere when he tells the Count's representative that he is primarily interested in the Count's daughter rather than in the amount of the dowry?
12. Why does the Duke call his visitor's attention to the statue of Neptune taming a sea horse? How do the two final words "for me!" complete the picture the entire poem has been creating of the Duke's character?

RANKING OF DISCUSSION

From this discussion, teachers in one variation ranked the discussion performance of the students, focusing on degree of participation (contributing), relevance (staying on topic), clarity (including evidence), and collaboration (asking questions, brevity).

T a s k 3: Analysis of Dialogue in Literature

First, read "My Last Duchess," then write a composition in which you present what you imagine the Count's envoy–that is, his representative or go-between–might report to the Count about his visit with the Duke. Since the envoy is silent throughout the poem and since the poem tells little about the Count, you will have to use your imagination in determining what the two men were like, what their relationship was, and then what questions your imagined Count would be likely to ask of your imagined envoy and what answer your imagined envoy would be likely to give. Your major problem may be to decide just how honest the envoy will dare to be, but take into account all that the envoy has seen and heard, what his resulting impressions of the Duke must be, what he must realize the Duke is after, and how he must feel about the Duke's trustworthiness. Although you will have to use your imagination, keep your imaginings in line with what the poem has told you. This task focuses on Standard 3.

Exemplar High

To Be or Not to Be

"Good afternoon, Count," greeted the envoy, bowing low. "I have just returned from the Duke's palace. It was indeed a thing of beauty. The treasures held in his possession were varied and valuable. Your daughter would have all the valuable items to see every day and show off to guests when entertaining. One such treasure was a statue of Neptune taming a sea-horse . . . there is a message in that statue." This last was murmered so low that the Count could scarcely hear it.

"What's that you say?" demanded the Count.

"Oh, nothing, sir, I was just clearing my throat. To continue, the Duke had a magnificent picture of his last Duchess. She looked so lifelike, almost as if she would begin to talk and breathe in the next moment. Fra Pandolph has done a masterpiece."

"All this is very well, very well," said the Count irratably. I know all about the Duke's priceless wonders. What I wish to know is what you, personally, thought of the Duke as a match for my daughter. You have been in my service a long time, and your opinion is valued highly."

The envoy hesitated, as if searching for the right words.

"Well, sir, I would say he is a man of the world, well-versed in antiques and knowing the correct clothes to wear and the art of conversation. He seemed proud of his name and all the things that lay behind it."

"Yes, yes, I know all that. But what I want to know is your opinion of the Duke. Do you think he will be a good match for my daughter?"

Again the envoy hesitated. Then, as if he had come to a decision, he heaved in a deep breath, squared his shoulders, and started in:

"Personally, sir, I was very impressed with the Duke. At the beginning when he showed me all the treasures I said to myself, 'What a fine match this would be. The Count's daughter will bask in all these glories. Then suddenly, when the Duke was showing me his last Duchess's painting, a change came over him. The model loving Duke became a beast, not so much by his actions as by the implication behind his words. He indicated that he was ashamed of her. I got the impression he was a callow person. He seemed to want your daughter's dowry first, next your daughter. That, sir, is my opinion."

With that the envoy bowed quickly and left the room.

T a s k 4: Writing Dialogue

First, read "My Last Duchess, then try writing a composition in which you have a single speaker reveal himself or herself solely by what he or she says–perhaps by what he or she leaves unsaid. Provide this speaker with both an occasion and a hearer–probably an audience of one. Through the speaker's words make clear to the reader the situation, the character of the speaker, and the relationship between the speaker and the audience. Make every word contribute to the reader's understanding of the speaker's character. This task focuses on Standard 5.

C o m m e n t a r y

This student's reconstruction of a scene, which we can only guess at by reading between the lines of the poem, is lively, dramatic, and imaginative. Both the envoy and the Count emerge in the course of the dialogue. The reader senses the relative social positions of the two men without the writer's stating it—or needing to. The reference to the statue of Neptune taming a sea horse is one of several unexpected insights in this tenth-grade paper, and one of the deftest touches is the envoy's insistence that he was only clearing his throat. The attempt to emulate the courtly formality of Browning's own language, the energy of the dialogue, the linkage to actual details in the poem, the avoidance of any violation of probability—all mark this as a high-range paper.

T a s k 5: Analysis of the Cumulative Sentence

The students were asked to imitate sentence models (taken from *An Occurrence at Owl Creek Bridge* by Ambrose Bierce) and produce their own cumulative sentences. This task, from Kathy Cocetti in Thornton, Colo., focuses on Standard 6.

MODEL SENTENCE

The other bank of the stream was open ground—a gentle *acclivity* topped with a stockade of vertical tree trunks, loopholed for rifles, with a single embrasure through which protruded the muzzle of a brass cannon commanding the bridge.

Exemplar High

The open clearcut alongside the trail stood obscurely vulnerable - a man-made plain covered with a sea of lush, dense groundcover, picked clean of berries, containing a lone juniper bush off which dined a six-point whitetail buck surveying the scene.

Exemplar Low

The other side of the pool had deep blue water --- a gentle breeze slapped the clear, crisp water, filled with with waves, a single cloud in the sky which drifted, then made a perfect umbrella to us all day.

MODEL SENTENCE

The humming of the gnats that danced above the eddies of the stream, the beating of the dragonflies' wings, the strokes of the spiders' legs, like oars which had lifted their boat—all these made audible music.

Exemplar High

The howling of the wolves that stood stoically on the peak of the outcrop, the rustling of the aspen leaves, the crashing of the ungulates' hooves, like the thunder of a brewing storm — together they defined the ineffable harmony of the wood.

Exemplar Low

The swaying of the trees that whistled slightly above the ripples in the creek, the clashing of the sky's under, the flashing of the frightening lightening, like a camera which had recently taken a picture - all these ended a savaging summer.

T a s k 6: Understanding Sentence Conventions & Structure

The following sentences were selected from a language task developed by the College Board as an end-of-year assessment for 10th graders. Students were given about twenty-five minutes to complete the task, which focuses on Standard 6.

The advantages of this kind of language question are the chances it offers for variety, range, and novelty in the items themselves; the demands it makes upon the active thinking and active writing skill of the student; and the fact that this kind of task avoids confronting the student with bad writing. The fifth sentence is the only piece of really weak writing in this task, and this sentence is here because the ability to spot and eliminate wordiness is important. Rewrite each sentence according to the directions which follow it and make as few changes as possible.

— Georgia was elected president of her class because of several characteristics. (Enumerate several of Georgia's characteristics without making a second sentence or changing what is already written.)
— If you ever dare to come into my nice clean kitchen again with those muddy boots, your father's going to hear about it. (Rewrite, making the sentence a gentle plea instead of an angry threat.)
— All the students who plan to attend the dance must buy their tickets in advance. (Change *All the students who* to *Each of the students who*.)
— If Ruby had had more practice diving, she would have been awarded the medal. (Rewrite, changing *If* to *Because* and keeping as close as possible to the meaning of the given sentence.)
— The teacher was pleased that for once each and every single one of all her students had punctually handed in on time his or her book report on Catherine Bowen's biography of the life of Justice Holmes. (Rewrite, cutting out all unnecessary words.)
— While Jordan was shopping in the square, a peddler sold him a Turkish rug. (Change *While Jordan was shopping* to *While shopping*.)
— For successful teaching, knowledge of the subject should be linked with the desire and ability to share that knowledge. (Rewrite, changing *For successful teaching* to *To be a successful teacher*.)
— Divide the money between the Girls' Athletic Association and the Boys' Service Club. (Add *and the Students' Publication Committee*.)
— Springfield is the capital city of Illinois. It is the burial place of Abraham Lincoln. (Change to one sentence, omitting one *is* and not using a conjunction.)
— The burglar's final shot missed its target and embedded itself in one of the ancestral portraits, improving it beyond all recognition. (Change the tone of this sentence by altering *one* word.)

SCORING DIRECTIONS

Each of the items in this question required anywere from one to four changes in the student's revision according to the given directions. The scoring system below indicates each of the required changes for each of the sentences. The student got one point of credit for successfully making each one of these changes. If in the revision, however, the student introduced errors not in the original sentence, the total score for the item was lowered by one point for each newly created error.

— 3-2-1-0 points as follows: 1 for any acceptable introduction of the series, either by a colon or by an expression like *such as, the following, some of which were,* etc.; 1 for correct punctuation of a series of at least three; 1 for parallel structure in the series.
— 2-1-0 points as follows: 1 for the introduction of the *please* idea; 1 for the elimination of the father as a threat.
— 2-1-0 points as follows: 1 for leaving *plan* unchanged; 1 for changing *their* to *his or her*.
— 2-1-0 points as follows: 1 point for correct sequence of tenses; 1 point for the use of the two negatives needed to keep the sense of the original contrary to fact condition.
— 3-2-1-0 points for eliminating the wordiness in each of the following: "each and every single," "punctually . . . on time," "biography of the life of."
— 2-1-0 points as follows: 1 for avoiding a dangling construction; 1 for avoiding passive voice.
— 1 point for avoiding a dangling infinitive phrase.
— 2-1-0 points as follows: 1 point for correct punctuation of a series; 1 point for changing *between* to *among*.
— 1 point for making an appositive out of either the idea of the capital or the idea of the burial place of Lincoln, with commas before and after the appositive.
— 1 point for changing *improving* to damaging, defacing, marring, destroying, or any other suitably sober term.

EDITORS

Miles Myers received his B.A. in rhetoric, his M.A. in English and M.A.T. in English and education, and Ph.D. (Language and Learning Division) at the University of California–Berkeley. He has served as the Executive Director of the National Council of Teachers of English since 1990, and has been president of the Central California Council of Teachers of English (in the 1960s), a vice president of the California Association of Teachers of English (in the 1970s), president of the Oakland Federation of Teachers-AFT (in the 1960s), and president of the California Federation of Teachers-AFT (in the 1980s). He was a co-director and the administrative director of the Bay Area, California, and National Writing Projects during the first ten years of their development (1975–1985), and for almost thirty years, he has been secretary-treasurer and later president of Alpha Plus Corporation, a nonprofit corporation of preschools in Oakland, California. He taught high school English for many years, primarily at Oakland High School, where he was department chair until 1975, when he left for the University of California–Berkeley. He taught English methods courses at the University of California–Berkeley for five years, at the University of Illinois Urbana-Champaign for three years, and at various other institutions for shorter periods of time. He was co-director of the literacy unit of New Standards, and he has served on the advisory boards of the Center for the Study of Writing at the University of California–Berkeley, the National Research Center on Literature Teaching and Learning at the State University of New York at Albany, and the Board on Testing and Assessment of the National Academy of Science. He has received the Distinguished Service Award from the California Association of Teachers of English, the Ben Rust Award for Service from the California Federation of Teachers-AFT, and an Exemplary Service Award from the California Council of Classified Employees. He has authored six books and monographs as well as many articles on the teaching of English.

Elizabeth Spalding received her B.A. in Latin and English and M.A. in Latin from West Virginia University, and her Ph.D. in Curriculum Studies and Language Education from Indiana University-Bloomington. She is assistant professor in the Department of Curriculum and Instruction at the University of Kentucky. Previously, she was Project Manager for Standards at the National Council of Teachers of English, where she worked on the NCTE/IRA project to develop K–12 content standards and managed the New Standards project to develop performance assessment tasks and a portfolio assessment system. She has conducted numerous workshops on portfolio scoring and other assessments. She taught high school English, French, and Latin for many years in West Virginia and in the Department of Defense Dependents Schools–Pacific Region. Her research interests include teacher perspectives, teacher education, and alternative assessment of literacy. She has authored several articles on alternative assessment and the experiences of novice teachers.